ULTIMATE GARAGE HANDBOOK

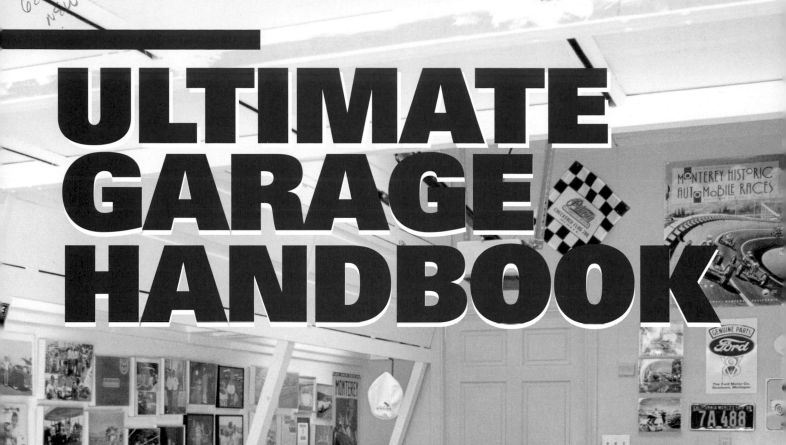

ULTIMATE GARAGE HANDBOOK

Richard Newton

MOTORBOOKS
INTERNATIONAL

First published in 2004 by MBI Publishing Company, Galtier Plaza, Suite 200, 380 Jackson Street, St. Paul, MN 55101-3885 USA

Motorbooks International titles are also available at discounts in bulk quantity for industrial or sales-promotional use. For details write to Special Sales Manager at Motorbooks International Wholesalers & Distributors, Galtier Plaza, Suite 200, 380 Jackson Street, St. Paul, MN 55101-3885 USA.

Library of Congress Cataloging-in-Publication DataAvailable
ISBN 0-7603-1640-6

Edited by Peter Bodensteiner & Lindsay Hitch
Designed by Chris Fayers

Printed in China

On the front cover: This roof was raised just over a foot to provide for more storage. *Michael Stewart*
On the title page: With this cantilevered truss system, the Porsche owner has created a great area for enclosed storage, and at the same time allowed himself room to move about. *Dennis Adler*
On the back cover: The floor in this garage is one huge expanse of plastic interlocking tile. The best part of this system is that you can create a unique design. *Mid America Motorworks*

CONTENTS

Introduction   6

Chapter 1: Planning Your Garage   9

Chapter 2: Building a Solid Floor   19

Chapter 3: The Challenge of Storage   30

Chapter 4: Workbenches   40

Chapter 5: Tools and Other Fun Things   48

Chapter 6: The Electrical Grid   62

Chapter 7: Let There Be Light   73

Chapter 8: Climate Control   82

Chapter 9: Wall and Ceiling Treatments   92

Chapter 10: Some Ideas from the Professional Shops   104

Index   111

INTRODUCTION

We all dream about the perfect garage, but few of us actually have one. Creating a great home garage isn't an easy task. The ultimate garage is an elusive target—your home changes, your family changes, and even your cars change. The poor garage just can't keep up with all of it.

It gets even more complicated when you realize that no one item will make the ultimate garage. All of the bits and pieces have to come together in a Zen-like fashion. Great lighting may be nice, but by itself you only end up with a very well lit, disorganized garage. A well-lit pile of dirty car parts will never be very attractive.

You might finally put a beautiful garage together only to find that when the temperature gets below freezing, you can't work in it for more than an hour. In comes the kerosene heater and your whole concept starts to fall apart. If you live in Florida, during July your beautiful garage turns into a well-organized sauna.

It is difficult to have a garage that is both functional and attractive at the same time. This is the mission of everyone that has ever built a shop or garage. The Ferrari dealer is looking just as hard for that magic combination of beauty and function.

Good garages don't just happen. You have to take some time and plan them. You have to decide what it is that you want to do in your garage. If you like to detail your car, then you need to pay a great deal of attention to the lighting arrangement. You won't need a great deal of storage, but you may need a home entertainment center to keep yourself amused while you attempt to remove every single bit of evidence that the car has ever been driven on a road.

If you plan on doing a major restoration, you'll need to pay particular attention to the types of storage available. It's amazing how much space a car can take up once it's apart. Keep in mind that you may very well have those parts sitting on the shelf for several months, even years. That means you're also going to have a dust and dirt problem. A lot has to be taken into consideration when you begin your design.

Then we come to the issue of cost. The garage itself is a sort of restoration project, and we all know that restoration projects often take on a life of their own and costs can spiral out of control. The cost of a nice garage will exceed all of your early estimates, just as it probably did with your last car project. What began as a gallon of floor paint from Home Depot may very well end with the installation of a 42-inch flat screen television and surround sound system.

A GARAGE IS MEANT TO BE USED

This may be a novel concept, but I truly believe that you should work on cars in a garage. Over the years, I've seen numerous garages featured in magazines and chronicled in books, but very few of these garages are used for working on cars. Most of them are simply very elaborate storage areas. Except for the elaborate flooring and expensive trim, they might as well be storage facilities.

No one ever actually works on cars in these garagemahals. I've even known people that have cocktail parties in their garages. That won't happen any time soon in my garage—people might actually get dirty. The emphasis in this book, then, is on how to combine comfort, appearance, and utility all in one space.

I've been in enough shops to know that you can combine function with design. It doesn't have to be a choice between the two. There is no need to have a cluttered shop just because you actually work on cars. I've heard that excuse too many times. On the other hand, your garage may never be an appropriate setting for a cocktail party, either. Remember, the goal here is to have a safe, clean, and comfortable place to work on cars.

EVERY GARAGE IS DIFFERENT

No two garages are the same. By necessity, each garage is a personal statement. Some are created from wood framing and others are constructed from concrete blocks. Some garages have windows and others have none. The only common elements that all garages share are a floor and walls. And most of them have roofs, but I've worked in a few that barely even had that.

When you restore a car today, it's mostly a matter of getting out the judging manuals and following them to the letter. Restoration is now a craft, with little or no artistry left. The same is true of racing. The rule books are getting bigger, but there is less and less creativity involved. There's no rule book for your garage. Your friends will judge your efforts without a manual to guide them. There will be no points deducted if you paint the floor red. Everything in your garage is open to your personal interpretation. You build it to meet your own needs and your own sense of aesthetics. It may well be the last frontier of automotive creativity.

GARAGES FOR REAL PEOPLE

One of the goals of this book was to come up with some ideas that the average car nut could use. Most of us are the basic two-, or maybe three-, car family, and most of us have a problem working on our toys in a home that was designed for raising a family.

I tried to keep in mind the person who needs help with the one-, or two-, car collection. If you own more than a half dozen collector cars, then you're on your own. Besides, you can probably afford a garage that is far beyond the ideas in this book.

Griot's Garage

One of the nice things about a garage project is that you don't need to spend a lot of money. The average home garage renovation is usually not a major cash project, it's just a lot of hard work and planning. You can make a tremendous difference for around $500. If you've got $1,000, you can make a real difference.

The condition of your current garage is a major budgetary factor. If you have bare walls and minimal electrical service, the project is obviously going to cost more than one that is of fairly recent vintage. The final cost will be determined by where you start.

SOME RESOURCES

At the end of each chapter, I've included a couple of resources to help you in your madness. The single most important resource you may have is Google. Less than half a dozen books have been written about the home garage, and none even come close to helping build the Ultimate Garage. Use Google and the Internet to fill in the gaps.

You're going to have to search out every aspect of your renovation and think creatively about how things can be twisted and revised to fit your needs. Just as no one understands why you would spend a bunch of money and even more time on an old car, no one understands what you really need in a garage.

SHOP TILL YOU DROP

Before you start this project, you should spend about six months wandering the aisles of Home Depot and Lowe's. Don't buy anything right away. Just become familiar with what's out there. Every day, new home improvement products are invented. People like us figure out new ways to use these products.

Any number of kitchen and bathroom products, not to mention ideas, can be transformed into garage items. The truth is, most kitchen and bath products are of a far higher quality than what is offered for the garage. Lighting systems are the prime example; floor coverings are another.

Each aspect of your garage project offers a myriad of choices. Don't stick to the traditional garage products. For example, I love Restoration Hardware for cabinet trim and handles. They're far superior to anything offered in the traditional garage product lines.

Your garage is small enough that you can upgrade things for small amounts of money. No matter what you're doing to your garage, the expense difference between economy products and the top of the line is really minimal.

IT'S NEVER FINISHED

Your garage is never complete. No matter what you've done up to this point, there are still improvements that can be made. And just when you think you have it all finished, something changes. You get a new car, or worse yet, the kids get new bikes. Then your teenage son decides he really needs a riding lawn mower for the family estate.

Now it starts all over again. You really can't think of your garage as a project. It's more like a journey. The fun comes from stopping along the journey and reflecting on how far you've traveled.

Your garage is a journey that will introduce you to new products and new techniques. New ideas will strike you just as you make your final decisions, and that's not a bad thing. Just keep moving toward the goal of having the garage you've always dreamed about. It's all about turning these dreams into a reality.

DECIPHERING THE INFORMATION BOXES

At the beginning of each project you'll find a list of topics and icons. This is a guide to help you decide whether to tackle a project or leave it for another time—or hire a professional. The info boxes will give you a good idea of what's involved and what you'll need in the way of tools, knowledge, and money. The list is self explanatory but just in case you're curious about how I arrived at these thoughts I'll break it down for you.

Time: Time is a rough estimate of how long the project would take a person with reasonable skills and knowledge. I generally estimate that everything I do in my garage will take twice as long as I originally thought and that sort of thinking will get you in the ballpark.

Tools: For the simple projects, I listed the wrenches and even the sizes you might need. For the advanced projects, the list would be longer than the project description so I've only listed the specialty tools. Remember that no matter how extensive your tool collection, you'll make trips to the store more often than you can imagine. Include the cost of new tools in the budget for a given project.

Talent: Be honest with yourself about your abilities. Garage projects involve every possible craft and none of us are good at all of them. If a project has one icon, anyone can give the project a shot. Two icons mean that you should be proficient with tools. At the third level, you should have experience with a similar project and know how to do things with little guidance. At the fourth level, you should be extremely handy and own a lot of tools. At the very least you need to know where to rent the specialized tools and who to ask for advice. Generally these jobs are best left to the professional—or the very brave.

Tab: The tab is a ballpark idea of how much money you'll to spend. Over the years, I've developed a formula to budget for any project. Look up all the prices for materials and tools while you're roaming the aisles at the home improvement store. Make a fairly detailed list of all the items and prices; now take that total and double it. The final amount will be fairly close to what you'll end up spending. Every project takes on a life of its own and will exceed your preliminary budget at least twofold.

This wonderful floor—gray enamel floor paint —was cheap and easy to put down. Alex Job moved into the building three years ago and needed flooring that was not only easy to install, but would also allow them to get the shop up and running as quickly as possible. They had a tremendous advantage in that the floor was brand-new concrete.

CHAPTER 1
PLANNING YOUR GARAGE

ost garages just happen. You move into the house, and then one day you start getting your car tools out. Maybe you get the bikes and the fertilizer spreader out first, but eventually you're going to choose a place for your tools. Over the years, you add some more car tools, more cars, and unfortunately more lawn tools.

After a while, all of the stuff gets jumbled together and you have an array of cabinets, workbenches, and shelving and a garage that could have appeared on *Sanford & Son*. Every time you start a project, a few more parts get moved around. Before you know it, you can't find anything.

Then one day you finally decide something has to happen. It may be the day the bike falls over on the Porsche,

or the day when you back the Chevelle with the original factory tires over a rake, but it is a day you'll remember.

The problem is that you've done this before. A few years back, you moved half your tools to the other side of the garage and thought that was the solution. How long did that last? Not long. This time we're going to do a total rehab.

THE LOOK—WHAT IS IT?

When planning your garage, you'll need to decide on the look you want to create. Just as your wife strives for a certain look in her part of the house, you want your garage to look a particular way. Currently, the high-tech race car look is very popular. The basement rec room look, complete with a wet bar, is another popular look today. These are the two ends of the garage spectrum.

Your garage will be a compromise somewhere between these two extremes. Roger Penske has never had to decide where to put the fertilizer spreaders at his shop in Reading. We, on the other hand, have to deal with a variety of issues regarding what belongs (and what doesn't belong) in our garage.

I've often thought that if you own a Ferrari it should be mandatory to have the floors constructed of Italian tile. An older Porsche, on the other hand, would best be served with a lot of oak workbenches and hand-fabricated wooden tool-

Most garages lack natural light. We get so carried away with security issues that we forget how nice it is to have natural sunlight flowing into the garage.

More and more garages are being built with a desk in the garage. As the computer becomes an integral part of the garage, you're going to need a place to put it. You also need a place to hide all your parts bills.

Here's a basic sound system in a garage. You can upgrade the home entertainment center in your home "because you have such a wonderful family." Then quietly move the old stuff into your garage. You could just purchase new stuff for your garage, but then you'd have to explain to the family why the 50-inch plasma screen is better in your garage than in the living room.

I prefer having two extinguishers in the garage. Place one on each side wall. If you're working on a fuel system, place it on the floor right next to you.

boxes. I'm not sure what to do with British cars. Perhaps you could build a metal Quonset hut in your backyard. On the other hand, a floor constructed of paving bricks might look appropriate, too.

Having said all this, I have to admit that my current garage is best described as a college dorm room. There are some very nice things hidden amongst the clutter, but your first impression would be the same one your parents had when they first visited your college dorm.

The point I'm trying to make is that nice garages don't just happen. They take some planning. Remember, the garage, at least to you, is the most important room in the house. Give it some serious thought.

WHAT IS SPACE?

Think about space. What is space? How many dimensions are there in space? Your garage is a cube, or more correctly, a rectangular solid. Your cars are also solids. Let's think about the total space in the average two-car garage. It's normally a 20-foot by 20-foot box that's around 8 feet tall. That means your garage is roughly 3,200 cubic feet of space.

Now think about your cars. They usually run about 15 feet in length and about 5 or 6 feet in width. Remember, you want enough room to get in and out of the car. These fairly substantial rectangular solids, or cars, take up a lot of space in your garage. That's not all bad. After all, the purpose of the garage is to house these cars. It's not the garage's

fault that you want to do a whole lot more than just park cars in it.

You may be able to arrange your cars in a slightly different manner to free up some space on the edge of your garage. Later in this chapter, we'll look at parking cars sideways in the garage in an effort to make more room. If your garage is a box, you need to think outside of this box. There's a tremendous amount of space on all of your walls and along the ceiling. The real trick is to use all of the space that's available to you and then light the space.

Begin by measuring the floor space that you have in your garage. This is the space you have to work with. In the old days, when we moved into the house, we drove a couple of cars into the garage and built a workshop around them as best we could. Then the family changed. The kids got new bikes, and the wife bought an SUV. But you're not going to take it anymore; this time you're going to do it right.

SOME CHOICES TO THINK ABOUT
Additions

You may want to consider adding another section on to your current garage, although this isn't always possible. A lot of us live in communities that restrict the size of garages. In many of the new communities, it's just not possible to add space to your current garage. On the other hand, if it's at all possible, it's something that you need to consider when you start your planning.

I'm more impressed with the pit in this garage than I am with the TV in the back cabinet. The nice thing here is the cover that goes over the pit. If you copy this example, make sure that the cover is solid and is held securely in place. The last thing your insurance company needs to hear is that you fell in your garage pit. That would be an interesting conversation. Phil Berg

Also give some thought as to how this addition can be used. Don't assume that you will simply add another bay in parallel to the two or three you already have. You can run an addition perpendicular to the others you have. You may not even need a driveway if you don't use this particular car every day of the week. Get creative.

With an addition, your electrical system can simply be extended into the new area. A totally new garage takes a lot more effort. When you build a new structure you have to make provisions for electrical systems and maybe even water systems. When you add on to your existing garage, you can simply extend the current facilities. This is a real advantage.

A Brand-New Garage

You may decide to give up on the current garage and deed it over to your wife and children and put a new place out back. This option requires some extra property surrounding your house. Most of us can't even consider an additional building functioning as a shop because the basic suburban lot is not big enough for yet another three-car garage.

The beauty of this separate-garage solution, though, is that you can start from the beginning. You can spend a lot of time thinking about what you really want in a garage and then make it a reality. Another advantage of a totally new garage is that it's a stand-alone unit. This garage can become your own personal haven. Everything can be part of a self-

Here is another example of a garage pit. These are a great alternative to the cheap lifts sold in enthusiast magazines. They don't cost much more than a lift and they're far more convenient. A garage pit is nothing more than a hole in the ground, so make sure you have adequate lighting. Phil Berg

contained unit. Not only can all of your prized possessions be kept in one place, but other things, such as bicycles and gardening tools, can be kept out of this personal space.

The downside of having a stand-alone unit is that you're going to have to run electrical and water lines to your new sanctuary. This not only adds to the cost but also to the

We probably don't use sliding doors enough; we've become too accustomed to the ubiquitous overhead door. Sliding doors take up no space on the ceiling. The overhead garage door is extremely convenient, but you should consider some other type of door for places where you store collector cars. Bill Delaney

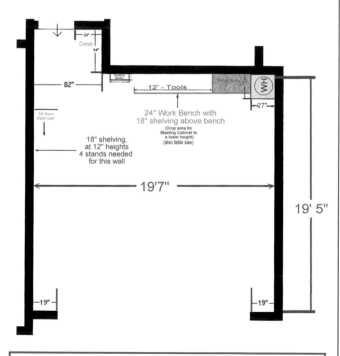

One really great way to plan your garage is to use your computer to construct a drawing. You can play with all of the numbers until your heart's content; just make sure that your measurements are correct.

Start your planning early in the construction process. If you're building a new home, make sure to request all the appropriate wiring and flooring options. Then it's just a matter of adding your details to the space when you move in.

complexity of the project. A totally new structure means creating a whole new infrastructure of heating, plumbing, and electrical systems.

If this stand-alone unit is large enough, your municipal government may treat it as a commercial structure. If the structure *could* be used as a commercial space then many local governments will treat it as a commercial space. This includes all of the requirements for the electrical, heating, and plumbing systems. Be prepared for this as you build your new fantasy garage.

A Storage Shed?

Every home center has a wide selection of small storage sheds for your property. These sheds can help you get a lot of stuff out of your garage, but they're pretty ugly and a lot of communities are banning them.

However, the beauty of these sheds is that you can finally get all of the nonessential nonsense out of your garage, although you shouldn't phrase it that way to your family. It's better to say that they now have their own space for bikes and sporting equipment. Then one day simply sneak all the gardening equipment into the shed and you're on the way to the perfect motor madness garage.

It would be foolish to construct your own shed since so many varieties are available. Your time is better spent land-scaping the area around the shed so the neighbors don't have a coronary.

Stuff You Really Don't Need

If you look around your garage, you're going to find a lot of stuff that belongs to the rest of the family. Your first inclination is to simply chuck all of this stuff, but you know you

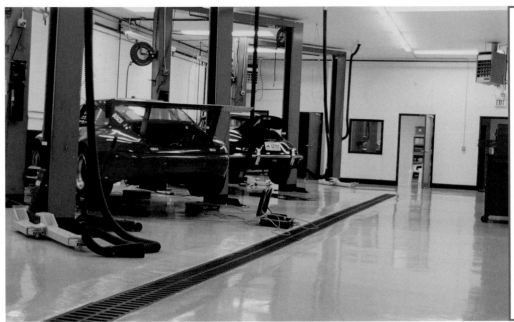

These are some serious lifts. They cost almost twice as much as the little toys you see advertised in the enthusiast magazines. And look at how the bays are placed on an angle with a driveway behind them. This arrangement is pretty common in commercial shops. There's no reason why it can't be used in a home garage—a big home garage. It would be ideal to have a rectangular garage with one single overheard door at the end. Precision Epoxy Products

can't do that. After all, you are simply one member of the family. Right now, the family tolerates your car hobby. If you restrict access to their toys, you could be in a heap of trouble.

All of the bikes and sports equipment need to be considered. You need to make sure that the family has access to them, and at the same time, make sure that they're not in a place where they can do damage to your cars or equipment.

The other question is how much of your stuff do you really need? Take some time to review your collection. Do you really need those old Mustang tires with the cracked sidewalls? Do you really need the two extra rear deck lids for your 911? Remember, at some point in your life, your kids are probably going to throw a lot of this stuff out anyway. Get a head start on it for them.

A LOOK AT SOME PLANS

Most of us don't have the luxury of building a new garage. Nonetheless, it doesn't hurt to look at a variety of plans to see how other people have organized their space. All of these plans are essentially blank canvases that allow you to create a personal statement.

Each of the four plans on the next three pages offers a slightly different concept for a garage. The overall dimensions can be changed

to suit your needs and the amount of property you have available. Everyone with a car addiction has the same problem—what do I do with everything I own?

You can get some great ideas from looking at garage plans. Do you have room for a loft? Can you install a shop area in front of the cars in your current garage? I haven't seen a garage yet that didn't have at least one idea I could steal.

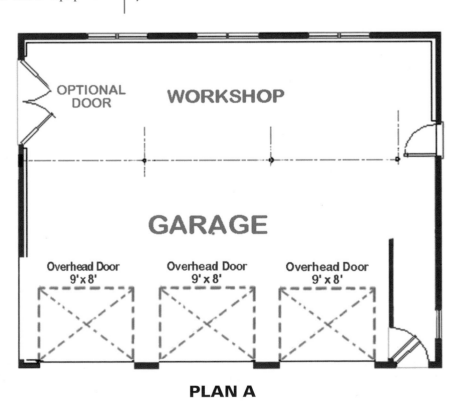

PLAN A

Plan A—The Monster Garage

This is the biggest and possibly one of the best designs out there. A space this large allows for a wide range of options. The problem is that the footprint is huge. You're going to need a lot of land for this garage, but it could solve a lot of problems. The most important feature of this garage is the area in the rear.

The rear area can be used as a giant workshop, or it can be a place to park your car trailer, with the car still in it. This way you can keep your trailer nice-looking without having to put a lot of effort into cleaning it every time you want to go some-place.

In this case, something other than an overhead garage door would be best. Overhead doors are fantastic for going in and out, but they take up a serious amount of ceiling space. Conventional swinging, or even sliding, doors are much better for the workshop area. These doors will be used so seldom that it's worth considering the alternative to the ubiquitous overhead door.

Alternatively, this rear space can be used for a complete machine shop. This will finally allow you to operate that Bridgeport vertical mill you couldn't pass up at the auction. You might even develop a polishing center in a space this large. Imagine having an array of buffing wheels all mounted on very solid pedestals.

The other nice feature is that your wife can still put her car in the garage. There's enough room for everyone's car in this garage, at least until your teenagers start to drive.

The major advantage of a monster garage is that you only need one system for everything; this includes electrical and heating and cooling systems. You only have to insulate one structure and only have one roof to repair 25 years from now.

Plan B—A Basic Large Garage

This is your basic oversized two-car garage. It's all on one level and the space is totally open. Think of this garage as a bare palette. Even if you already have a garage that's similar to this, start your design as if it's totally empty.

This plan gives you 780 square feet of space to work with. After you drive two cars in the garage, you still have over 300 square feet to use for a shop or storage. Only about half of the garage is used for parking cars.

PLAN B

STORAGE AREA
22' x 4"

2 BAY GARAGE
22' X 22'

WORK SHOP
8' x 26'

30'

26'

Overhead Door
9' x 7'

Overhead Door
9' x 7'

The downside here is that you can still only get two cars in this garage. If you're involved in a restoration project, you could park a third car back in the corner, but it would have to be a small car.

This plan can be used as an attached garage or a stand-alone unit. One nice feature of this garage is there is a separate door for coming in and out of the garage. Without this door, you would have to raise and lower the large garage doors every time you went in and out of the garage. If your garage has a climate control system, you lose all of your heat or air conditioning every time you go in and out of the garage.

Consider totally separating the workshop from the rest of the garage. This can be done with a simple partition, or you can actually convert the workshop area into a separate room. That would give you a workshop with over 200 square feet and only that 200 square feet would require a climate control system. That could save you a lot of money on your electric bills. It would also mean the smaller space would heat up quickly—not a small consideration if you live in upstate New York.

Plan C—A Garage with a Loft

The beauty of having a loft in your garage is the tremendous storage space you acquire. This option really isn't

PLAN C

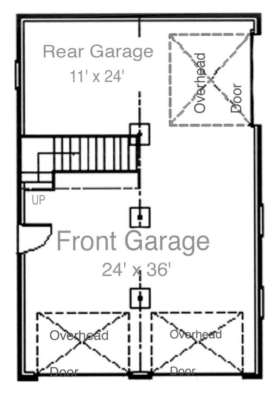

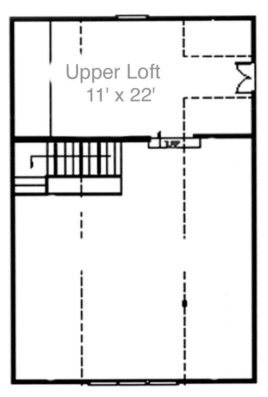

First Floor Plan   Loft Floor Plan

considered enough. We've all used attics above the garage for storage, but no matter how nice that area may be, it's still an attic.

A loft is much more open. Not only can you stand up and walk around in a loft, but you have adequate lighting. Those two items alone put the loft in a whole different category than the garage attic. A loft design also takes up a lot less space on your property. You get a tremendous amount of square footage with a relatively small footprint on your property. There is no other way to increase your usable space by 50 percent and still keep the building the same size.

The plan shown here is for an oversized three-car garage. This plan assumes that you really only drive two of your cars on a regular basis and allows the third (and possibly fourth) car to sit in the rear below the loft.

The downside to a loft is that you'll be moving a lot of parts from one floor to the next. You'll have to carry parts up and down a staircase or install a chain fall lifting system. You've probably already had to deal with a similar problem of getting stuff into your garage attic, but here you can simply run a beam out of the loft with a chain fall attached.

Climate control is another problem with this garage plan. There's a tremendous amount of ceiling space to heat and cool. Those of us who live in Florida or Texas will have

This solution calls for just giving up and putting your very own garage out back. The rest of the family can have the regular garage and you can create your own little garagemahal. Purchasing a prefab such as this is cheaper than having a contractor build one, but you'll probably need to spend money on landscaping to appease your neighbors.

15

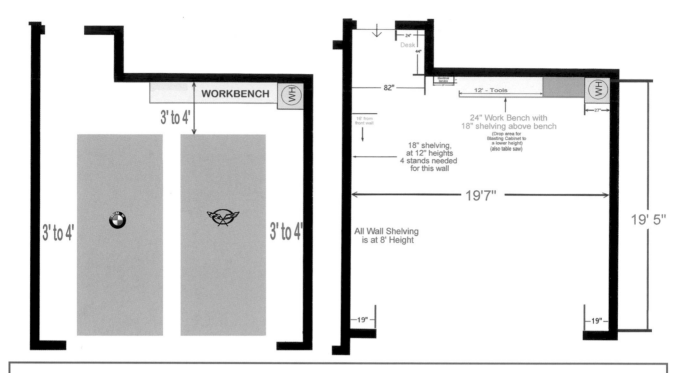

More than likely, this is your garage—a basic, all-American, 20-foot by 20-foot two-car garage with a universal overhead door and a remote actuator. This is hardly anyone's dream garage, but it's what most of us have to work with. If you put a Corvette and a BMW in this garage you've got a lot of room to work with. If you have a Ford Expedition you've got a problem. If you plan carefully, you can get a lot of things into the place. Both of the side walls can be used for storage and a small workbench area can be built in the front. The trick with this design is to run your shelving and cabinets from the floor all the way to the ceiling. That gives you a lot of storage even if it is a little difficult to access the top shelves.

A CHECKLIST FOR YOUR GARAGE

Storage and Work Areas
- Nothing is on the floor except for engines and transmissions. They are all placed on a dolly that allows them to be moved easily.
- Shelves, cabinets, pegboard, and overhead storage racks are all easily accessible.
- A solid workbench is located in the work area.

Heating, Cooling, and Ventilation
- Ductwork for heating and air conditioning have been considered and designed.
- Windows, fans, air conditioners, and space heaters all have a dedicated location.

Safety
- Anything that is flammable is stored away from heat.
- Dangerous chemicals, tools, and power equipment have been locked away from children.
- Smoke detectors and fire extinguisher locations have been selected.

Water Supply
- A utility sink has been installed for cleanup without using the family sink in the kitchen.
- All floor drains have been removed since toxic fluids can leak from a car and contaminate groundwater.

Walls and Floors
- Insulation has been planned for the walls and ceiling.
- The walls have been designed to reflect light.
- Vinyl baseboards have been planned to ease cleaning.
- The flooring has been selected and cost estimates are within the budget.

Lighting and Power
- Adequate lighting is designed for *both* work and storage areas.
- Electrical outlets are placed every 4 feet and at a comfortable height.
- Provisions have been made for 220-volt tools.

One alternative to garage clutter is to purchase a storage shed. Put it out back, landscape around it, and deed it over to the family. Make it sound like you're doing them a huge favor and then take back control of your garage.

real problems keeping cool in the summer. You folks in Minnesota are going to have a hard time keeping warm in January. It can be done, but you'll need to spend some extra money on a climate control system.

You don't necessarily have to build a new garage to get a loft. You might be able to simply raise the roof on your current garage. Be sure to hire a skilled engineer to look at your situation before you embark on this task. Raising the roof of your garage is not something that can be designed by the folks at Home Depot. Seek professional help on the design as well. Remember, you do have neighbors and, even more importantly, you might want to sell the house some day.

Plan D—The Shed

This hideaway garage is actually my favorite. While it's basically a shed, it's also a very personal space where you can go and play with your cars. This is the type of garage you need when you've finally surrendered to the rest of the family. They can keep the pool supplies, gardening supplies, and bikes in the normal attached garage, but you now have your own space to do whatever you want.

A self-contained space can be equipped without the usual considerations that you have to make in the family garage. It's a dedicated space where you can run electrical outlets and air lines to your heart's content.

The downside of this type of garage is that you'll have to run power, and maybe water lines, to the garage. This means that you'll need some professional help in the construction process, but it may be worth it.

FIRE SUPPRESSION SYSTEMS

Not many people think about this until it's too late. What happens if your garage catches on fire? How many cars will be lost and how much equipment will need to be replaced? If you have a fire in your garage, it's best to already have a plan in place. Thinking about how to save your car and actually putting out a fire are not things you want to do at the same time. Answer the following questions before something happens:

- Where are your fire extinguishers?
- Do you have smoke alarms installed?
- Are combustibles stored in a steel cabinet?
- Do you work on fuel systems with the garage door closed?
- How close is your battery charger to the combustibles?

These may seem like silly questions—that is, until you've had a fire. Remember, no one has ever planned on having a fire in their garage. But suddenly it can become a reality. When the fire hits all those little aerosol cans, they will explode like hand grenades. That's when the fire department becomes more concerned with its personal safety than your garage.

There are two minimum requirements for your garage. First, you should have a smoke detection system. Ideally, the system should be tied into your home system. Every home is different, but the important thing is to install a system that meets the particular needs of your home.

You also need at least one fully charged fire extinguisher. If you have a three-car garage, you should have two extinguishers. The day you have a fire it will start about as far away from the fire extinguisher as possible. Make sure they are easily accessible.

RESOURCES

There are two key items in your garage planning. The first is inspiration. You need to look at what is possible. Most of us are caught in the maze of the suburban American housing development. That means we have the basic two- or three-car attached garage.

A few of us are fortunate enough to have extra land for a whole new garage, and that's where the inspiration comes in. Look at several hundred plans and then let your imagination take it from there. Be creative. Be bold.

The next step is the actual design. Many companies offer detailed plans that include a materials list and complete specifications. This is where the dreaming stops and the hard work begins. The good news is that these companies have

THE WEEKEND PLAN

There are times when you really don't want to get involved in a major garage rehab project. For times like these, I came up with what I call the "Weekend Plan." In one weekend, you can make a major improvement to your garage. The key to this weekend project it to have everything you need on hand before you empty your garage into the driveway.

1. Clear It Out: First, you'll need to completely empty the garage. Set aside a Saturday when you are expecting good weather, and bring together as many helping hands as you can to lift, tote, and drag your belongings out into the driveway.

2. Sort Your Belongings: Sort things into three categories and do it right in the driveway. At the end of the day, you should have three piles. Call them Keep, Give Away (or Sell), and Throw Away.

3. Like Goes With Like: Now organize all the 'Keep' items into like groups, placing all sports equipment, tools, gardening equipment, automotive supplies, and painting supplies together in groups. If you're placing them in boxes, use clear plastic boxes or use stick-on labels and a permanent black marker. If they don't fit into boxes, place them in clear plastic bags.

4. Wall Space: Slotted panels called GearWall are a really quick way to cover the walls. They're part of the new Gladiator Garage Works organizing system from Whirlpool (www.gladiatorgarageworks.com). Wall cabinets can be mounted on to brackets that simply clip into the GearWall. Hooks and shelf brackets just snap into place. Heavy-duty equipment wall hangers allow multiple tools on one hanger. These hangers snap into grooves in GearWall and can be relocated anywhere, at any height. Garage Tek (www.garagetek.com) has a similar system.

5. The Floor: Large vinyl garage floor protectors from Better Life Technology can be rolled out, and then trimmed to fit using a utility knife (www.bltllc.com), for $2 a square foot. The floor itself should get some sort of wall-to-wall floor covering that provides an easy-to-clean surface. Try to keep as many items off the floor as possible so it's easy to sweep. You can use a canister-style vacuum to clean the garage floors after you have picked up the larger items with a broom.

6. Storage: You can quickly install new wheeled cabinets, with locks for hazardous chemical storage, for $200 to $500.

7. Workspace: Your new workbench should include wall cabinets, a solid maple worktop, three 24-inch-deep, pull-out cabinets with storage for both hand and power tools, and additional lighting above the bench.

already done the complex work, which can save you a tremendous amount of money and time.

Most of this information is available on the Internet and can be found through standard search engines. The sites listed below will get you started on the quest for the perfect motor madness sanctuary.

Cool House Plans
14 Savannah Highway, Suite 15
Beaufort, South Carolina 29906
800-482-0464
www.coolhouseplans.com
This is a wonderful site if you're planning on building a new garage. They can supply you with all the necessary blueprints. It's also a wonderful site to find ideas about garage layouts.

CAD Northwest Custom Home Design
9565 S.W. 69th
Portland, Oregon 97223
503-245-8974
www.cadnw.com
This site offers you a huge number of plans. They also offer a complete specifications list for all of their garages.

B4UBUILD.COM
10 Owl Branch Lane
Parkton, Maryland 21120-9522
410-329-6165
www.b4ubuild.com
This is a basic construction resource that points you toward all sorts of plans and resources. This should be one of your very first stops on the quest for the perfect garage. They have sample contracts, a planning center, plus a host of other things you'll need. This is a good first stop in the construction process.

The floor is the very first thing a person sees when they enter your sanctuary of motor madness. They may take note of your prized vehicle, but a great garage floor seems to make more of an impression than the car that's parked on it.

You can have all the Snap-on toolboxes in the world, but if you have a nasty floor, it's just another garage. There are dozens of solutions to flooring problems, and some of them actually work. I've tried most of these solutions with varying degrees of success. Some of these solutions are going to cost a lot of money while others are under $100. Over the years, I've discovered that cost has very little bearing on what actually looks good.

For the first six months, just about any flooring solution looks good. The real test is seeing what it looks like after three years. Endurance is more critical than how the floor looks initially. Garage floors take the same abuse as the pavement outside your home. You drive in and out of your garage as often as you use the driveway that leads up to it. The problem is that we want a garage floor that looks better than the kitchen floor, when in reality, the garage is just an extension of the driveway.

THE MOISTURE PROBLEM

Before you do anything, you need to see if you have a water migration problem coming from beneath the concrete floor in your garage. If your house was built properly, a vapor barrier was placed under the concrete floor prior to it being poured. This prevents any ground moisture from migrating from the soil into the concrete.

Since you probably weren't around when the concrete was laid, and the builder saved $10 by skipping the vapor barrier, it may not have been installed. If it wasn't, you could have big problems with your garage floor. As the moisture migrates out of the soil to the surface of your concrete floor, it will push anything out of the way. There is no paint, including the epoxy paints, that can stop nature.

Before you even think about your flooring choices, tape a 6-foot by 6-foot vinyl sheet down to your garage floor with duct tape. Leave this in place for about two weeks to see if you can trap any moisture under the vinyl.

If you find any moisture, your flooring choices are limited. Paint is simply out of the question. Installing vinyl tile will require the construction of a subfloor under the tile. Even carpeting is questionable since the moisture will attack the

This is one huge expanse of plastic interlocking tile. The best part of this system is that you can be creative with your design. Lay out a grid on paper to plan your creative exercise. Mid America Motorworks

When you want absolute perfection, epoxy floors are the best. You're looking at a poured epoxy floor in a NASCAR engine assembly area. This area must be kept spotless at all times. This epoxy floor is very easy to keep clean, and considering that it's a small area, the flooring wasn't too expensive. You might want to consider finishing a small area of your garage in this manner. Who says you need the same flooring in every part of your garage? Besides, doing just a small area will help you determine if you want to tackle the whole thing. Precision Epoxy Products

carpet backing. You may very well be a candidate for the temporary type of flooring produced by companies such as Kiwi.

FLOORING CHOICES
Carpet

Carpet was a popular choice a few years back, but it's really inappropriate flooring for a garage. There are two problems with carpeting. First, after you drive your car over it a few hundred times, it mats down and starts to look really ugly. Add some road salt and things get really bad. The other problem with carpeting is that if any area gets damaged, the entire carpeting must be replaced. You can't just touch up the damaged area. Well, you could, but pretty soon all the patches will make your garage look like something out of *The Beverly Hillbillies*.

Having said all that, I have to admit that I really like carpeting in certain areas of my garage. I put a strip of tough industrial carpeting down in front of my workbench and I love it. It's held up very well and is a good insulator against the cold concrete.

This may look like the temporary plastic tile used by race teams, but it's really a quartz floor. These are ground quartz crystals blended with polymer resins and color pigments. They're stronger than slate tiles and if they get chipped you can repair them using a simple resin mixture. These are not cheap, though, so you might want to order a sample tile before you do a whole floor. Griot's Garage

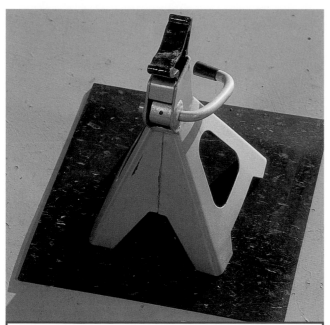

Once you have the perfect floor you need to protect it. Here, I'm using a cheap floor tile to keep the jack stand from scratching the floor. Most floor damage will come from using normal equipment in the shop.

Here is an example of tile flooring and a wheeled dolly that can be used to move a car around. Tile takes as much effort to clean as any other flooring surface. A car that doesn't get used very often, such as this Lola, can become a giant dirt collector. These dollies allow you to easily push the car out for cleaning and the dolly wheels don't leave an impression on the tile.

I also like the approach a friend of mine takes. He cleans his garage every two years, and I mean seriously cleans it. Every single item is moved to the driveway and the carpet is ripped up. After the walls are painted, a new layer of thin carpeting is installed in the garage. This lasts another two years.

Removable Tile

Interlocking floor tile is the latest thing to hit the garage world. The beauty of this tile is that when rainstorms hit, water simply runs right through the tile. Once the rain stops, the flooring is dry and everyone is happy. Kiwi was the first to offer this sort of interlocking tile, and Racedeck followed quickly with a similar product. But in your home garage, dirt and paint chips fall through the floor and take up permanent residence on the concrete slab. You can vacuum all you want, but you'll never get all the dirt up. The only solution is to remove all the tile from your garage and start over again. It's even worse if you spill brake fluid. Instead of simply wiping the fluid from the floor, you have to remove the tiles in order to get to the actual floor.

One nice feature of these tiles is that if you live in an area with snow and ice, water will flow out from under the tiles. Race teams began using interlocking tiles for their ability to allow water to drain quickly. The same thing works nicely in your home garage.

These tiles also come in colors so you can mark off certain areas of your garage. The tiles are perfect for

This is the best way to check for moisture in your garage floor. Unless a vinyl moisture barrier was installed under the concrete, you're going to have a problem with moisture migrating up through the concrete. Cut a sheet of vinyl about 6 feet by 6 feet and then duct tape it down. Leave it in place for about two weeks and see if you get any moisture buildup under the vinyl. If there's any moisture content, you will not be able to use paint on the floor. It also means that you won't be able to use vinyl adhesive tile without constructing a subfloor. If there is no moisture, there's a pretty good chance that you can use paint on the floor.

PROJECT 1 ★ *Tile Floor Installation*

Time: Several days

Tools: Brooms, trowels, chalk line

Talent: ★   **Tab:** $200–500

Tip: Take the time to make the floor underneath the tile as smooth as possible.

Tile only works when it's laid down on a good surface. Placed on a bad surface it will simply magnify the problems underneath. If there is a problem with the condition of the floor, take care of these floor problems before the tile actually goes down.

One solution is to install a plywood subfloor in the garage. Use a vapor barrier under the plywood and lay the vinyl tile on the plywood.

Vinyl Floor Tile Installation
- If your garage floor has been painted, make sure the old paint is firmly bonded to the floor. If you have a moisture problem, you're going to have to install a subfloor in your garage. Make sure that this floor is perfectly level and smooth.
- Tiles that require adhesive should never be used over paint. The adhesive will attack the paint and pretty soon you'll have a huge mess on your hands.
- Find the center point between the two longest parallel walls. Mark guidelines from the centers of opposite walls.
- Lay rows of tiles in both directions from the center without removing the adhesive backing. Adjust the tiles as necessary to balance the borders.

Laying the Tile
- Peel the backing paper from a self-adhering tile and place it at the center point.
- Make sure the tile is positioned correctly and then press down firmly.
- Lay all the tiles in a step fashion, starting in the center of the garage.
- Position the tiles so any arrows on the back all point in the same direction.

Using Adhesive to Lay Tiles
If you're installing tiles with adhesive the same cleanliness rules apply.
- Cover 1/4 of the garage with the adhesive.
- Allow the adhesive to "set" according to manufacturer's instructions and then place the tiles in a step fashion.

If your tiles have a directional arrow on the back, lay all tiles with the arrows pointing in the same direction. Once the tile is down it'll be too late to correct the mistake.

Fitting Partial Tiles
- To fit partial tiles; lay the tile to be cut exactly over the last full tile. Now place another full tile against the wall and mark the cutting line where the tiles overlap.
- Cut the tile on this line. Before removing the backing of self-adhering tile, check that the cut tile fits. Don't force it into place.
- Install the tile and press it firmly into position.

Finishing Up
- Immediately remove any excess adhesive from the tile surface using mineral spirits.
- When you complete the tile installation, roll the floor with a heavy roller to make sure all tiles are firmly stuck to the floor.
- Don't allow any water to get on the floor for five days. It's best to leave your cars outside for a week to let everything dry completely.

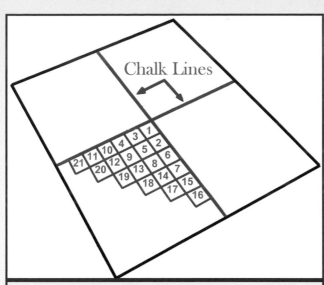

Chalk Lines

Tile the floor using quadrants. Divide your garage floor into four sections and tile one quadrant at a time. The key to this system is to make certain that you've found the center of the garage and that each quadrant is absolutely equal in size. Chalk lines are the best marking method. Measure everything a few times. You won't know if you've screwed up until you get to the edge of the garage. Just keep measuring and you should be fine.

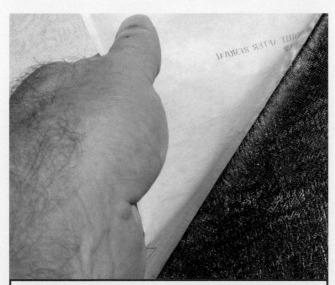

Self-adhesive tiles are the easiest way to put down a floor. Because of the sticky backing, there is no need to mess with gooey adhesives and seam sealers. Bring the tiles to room temperature by storing them in the garage overnight in open boxes. This is especially important when installing floors over concrete. The single most common mistake in any flooring project is applying the tile over a poorly cleaned or ill-prepared floor, or even worse, a garage floor that has a moisture problem.

motorcycles and small race cars, and if the area is small enough, you can pick them up and clean under them with minimal hassle.

Vinyl Tile

Vinyl tile is easy to lay down, easy to keep clean, and can be purchased at a number of local stores. But be aware that most vinyl tiles were never designed for use in a garage and aren't a very durable surface in an industrial setting. Be very careful with equipment on vinyl; it often leaves impressions in the tiles.

There are different types of vinyl tile. The tile you purchase at Lowe's or Home Depot is designed for home use. There's another type of tile designed for commercial use. Find a store that specializes in industrial and commercial tile before you make a purchase.

Moisture that seeps through your concrete floor can be as big a problem with vinyl tile as it is with paint. Armstrong tile even has specific recommendations for the maximum acceptable moisture emission levels for its installation.

Moisture attacks the tile's adhesive and causes it to soften, allowing the tile to slide. Tile installed over any moisture will expand slightly and later, when the concrete dries, the tile will return to its original size creating a gap. Excessive moisture can also cause the tile to curl at the edges, which makes the tile appear to shrink.

Vinyl tile may actually require more floor preparation than paint. In some cases, you may have to lay down a subflooring of 1/8- or 1/4-inch outdoor plywood to ensure that you have a quality floor that endures.

PAINT

I hate paint. I've painted too many shop floors in my lifetime, and I've had problems with virtually all of them. I've read every warranty that's ever been written. They all sound great, but not a single one will reimburse you for all the time you spent preparing and painting the floor. What good is a warranty if it only provides you with more of the same product that caused the problem in the first place?

If you have moisture seeping up through the floor from below, there isn't a paint in the world that will stay in place. If your moisture test shows excessive condensation, don't even think about paint. You're left with either removable tile or a bare concrete floor.

When you drive your car in the garage, the tires are hot; they transmit this heat to the paint. The paint actually bonds to the tires, so the next time you back out of the garage, some of your painted floor drives off with you.

Epoxy Floors

Today, everyone is calling their paint "epoxy." True epoxy is a bisphenol-A liquid resin. Epoxy is basically a synthetic

One way to keep the paint from peeling off your garage floor is to use long strips of thin industrial carpeting under the wheels. Virtually all paint on the market will peel from hot tires driving on it. Carpet strips solve that problem and simply hosing them down in the driveway will keep them clean.

This floor has suffered from moisture migrating up from the ground beneath the concrete. There is no hope for a floor with this problem. Water comes up under the paint and pushes the paint right off the concrete. For this situation, temporary plastic tiles would be ideal. If you've painted your floor and it starts to look like this, scrape up as much of the peeling paint as you can and scrub the floor really well.

resin produced by the reaction of epichlorohydrin and bisphenol. It's not paint, and you can't clean it up with soap and water. Technically, there is no such thing as latex epoxy.

The long and short of this is that epoxy is not a water-based product. If you can clean up your tools with water, you're not using an epoxy. If you really want to use an epoxy on your home garage floor, you need to do a lot of investigative work. The only company currently offering a true epoxy for home use is Precision Epoxy Products.

The Polished Floor: A New Solution

Polished concrete floors have been common in industrial settings for decades but have seldom been used in the home garage. The idea is very simple. Just forget all about the various floor coverings and polish the bare concrete.

If you plan on having polished floors in a new home or garage, make sure you let the contractor know. That way they can smooth the floor as much as possible to minimize the polishing steps required.

If your garage has been used for a number of years, there may be some extra steps involved to get a polished surface. Typically, older floors require some surface preparation prior to polishing. You have to remove dirt, grease, coatings, or blemishes. Polishing won't get rid of grease spots. In fact, they'll only get more obvious.

If you have a really lousy floor, you'll have to pass on this option. Floors that are wavy, need extensive patching, or are extremely porous are not good candidates for polishing. An experienced contractor can usually determine a floor's suitability. Make sure that you have the contractor come out to your home before they give you an estimate.

Here's the completed job with the Lola in place. But now the Lola area looks so nice that I have to just keep going. It's always very easy to get started; the problem is figuring out where the project ends. What started out as a project to enhance an area of roughly 100 square feet ended up as an 800-square-foot project.

The installation of this tile only took about a half hour. I spent more time thinking about the color selection and design than I did on the actual tile installation.

To help solidify polished concrete surfaces, some contractors apply penetrating hardeners to the concrete after the first step of the grinding process. These products chemically react with the concrete to form a hard, crystalline structure. They also prevent dusting of concrete and offer extra protection from water staining.

Polished concrete floors will reflect a lot more light than any of the alternative floor coverings. Polishing can actually give concrete a look that's similar to polished marble or granite and you can even apply a stain to the concrete during the polishing.

FLOOR MAINTENANCE
Stain Removal

In a perfect world, you have a shallow metal pan under your car to catch dripping oil and fill the pan with sand, kitty litter, or sawdust to help absorb the dripping oil. Periodically, you throw the entire pan out and replace it with fresh material.

If you happen to spill oil or grease on the floor, you immediately apply an absorbent powder such as fuller's earth, cornmeal, or sawdust to absorb as much oil as possible, leave it on the stain for a few hours, and then sweep it up. You can also use kitty litter for the same purpose, although you'll have a dust problem if you don't clean it up right away.

Unfortunately, most of the time we're trying to remove oil and grease that's been on the floor awhile. Here's a list of some common approaches that people have tried with varying degrees of success. I've even tried combining a couple of them in sequences.

- Sprinkle dishwasher detergent (the dry powder) on the wet floor and let it stand a few minutes, then pour boiling water on the area, scrubbing with a stiff long-handled brush, and rinse with a hose.
- Dissolve a cup of trisodium phosphate in 1 gallon of hot water and pour the solution over the stained surface. Allow this solution to soak 15 to 20 minutes and then scrub with a stiff brush or broom. Rinse off with a hose. Don't use this technique on asphalt or let the solution run out onto your asphalt driveway.

Using a rotary nozzle instead of a standard "fan" nozzle can also increase the cleaning speed. To produce a fan pattern, standard nozzles deflect the water at an angle, which slows the water down. Rotary nozzles spin a direct water jet in a circular path which means the water leaves the nozzle with greater speed.

Although higher pressures may be required to remove tough contaminants such as paint and heavy tire skid marks, most power washing contractors agree that 3,000 psi will do the trick for almost all cleaning jobs.

Before you use the pressure washer, clean the most severely soiled areas. Soak these areas with a strong detergent and scrub with a brush or push broom. If you use the pressure washer, you can use a 0-degree oscillating wand tip.

The Proper Technique

- Position a 15-degree tip so that the fan spray pattern is almost horizontal.
- Work in 10-foot by 10-foot sections. Begin in a corner and work toward the garage door.
- Hold the wand within 12 inches of the floor so that the spray strikes the floor at a 45-degree angle.
- Flush the entire floor with hot water after the power cleaning, and then scrub the floor with a clean push broom while you rinse.

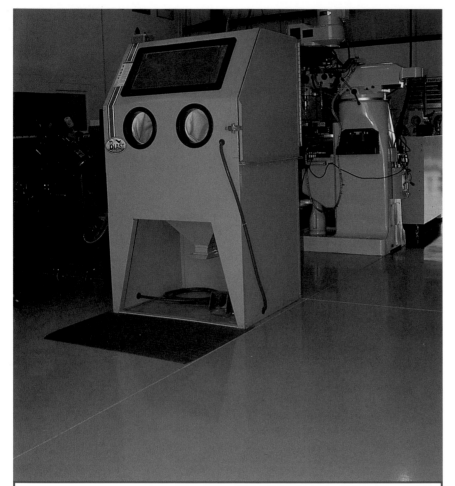

The beauty of a good floor is that it's easily cleaned. No matter how hard you try, sand will fall out of a blasting cabinet. Most of us stuff our cabinet into a corner where the dirt can hide for years. Alex Job Racing places their blasting cabinet in the center of the shop. With a perfect floor, a daily sweeping around the cabinet is all that's needed to keep the area clean.

- Mix one part sodium citrate to six parts water and six parts glycerin and add enough fuller's earth to make a thick paste. Spread this paste on the oil or grease stain. Let this solution stand for at least a week. Keep adding new paste as it dries. Flush with water after brushing the dry paste away.

Power Washing Your Garage Floor

There comes a time when you need to get really serious about cleaning your garage floor. You need to use a power washer with a pressure rating of at least 3,000 psi and a flow rate of at least 4 gallons per minute (gpm). To put this in perspective, look at the least expensive pressure washer at Lowe's. This unit does 2,350 psi at 2 gallons per minute. This unit retails for right around $300. Once you get above $1,000, you can find a unit that does 3,700 psi at 4 gallons per minute. A 13-horsepower Honda engine powers this unit.

- You can use fans, compressed air, or a leaf blower to reduce drying time. A squeegee helps to get the inevitable puddles out of the garage.

When everything is cleaned from pressure washing, you'll need to know how clean the floor really is. The best way to determine if the floor is clean is to spray water on a clean dry area. The water should flow evenly over the surface and actually wet the concrete. If the water beads or breaks, the surface is still contaminated and you'll need to do some more cleaning.

You can also check for invisible grease/oil in several areas of the floor by applying a 1:1 solution of muriatic acid to the floor. If the acid turns brown or does not react (bubble), grease/oil has penetrated the floor and a repeat degreasing procedure is necessary. Repeat the acid test after subsequent degreasing until all the areas tested indicate that the floor is free of grease and oil.

PROJECT 2 ★ *Floor Stain Removal and Power Washing*

Time: Several hours

Tools: Power washer

Talent: ★   **Tab:** $75–150

Tip: It's a lot easier to take care of stains as you create them rather than to let things form into an indestructible solid mass.

It's going to happen. Most likely it's already happened. Your garage floor has a massive stain. It needs to be cleaned up before anything else can be done. You can't paint over a stain, and you shouldn't even try laying tile over a stain.

The number one garage stain is oil. To make matters worse, it's the dirty oil dripping from your cars. Cars that show no sign of dripping are probably seldom driven. For those of us who actually drive our cars, oil stains are a fact of life.

Power washers are wonderful, but they take up valuable space in the garage and are only used once or twice a year. This new model is effective, but it's almost $200. Consider renting an even more powerful washer when you decide to clean your garage floor.

Kitty litter has been used to clean shop floors for years. It's still the best solution for bare concrete floors. The trick is to clean up the mess as well as you can with a cleanser and then use a brick to grind the kitty litter into the concrete. The dark stain will soon disappear, but you'll create a very fine pile of dust. If you use this technique sparingly, the dust is not a problem. Just don't try to do your whole garage floor this way.

27

If you have to put down a floor in your garage because of ground moisture migrating through the concrete here is the correct sequence: the asphalt underlay goes down first, followed by a heavy plastic sheet; 1/4-inch exterior plywood goes on top of the plastic; then start with the tile.

One of my favorite tricks is to use duct tape to determine how clean the floor is. Duct tape should adhere tightly to a properly degreased floor. If the tape doesn't tightly adhere, the presence of grease is indicated and further degreasing is necessary. Scrub that area a little harder.

Surface Preparation for Paint and Tile

Any new flooring has to stick to your old concrete floor. If you simply put new flooring down on top of your existing floor, then most of your problems will come back. A common reason for installing new flooring is that the old surface is coming up. You'll have to remove all of the existing coatings that are loose, peeling, or bubbling. Use pressure washing, hand scraping, and wire brushing to ensure that all of the old loose coatings are removed. I've even used large sanding discs on a power sander to get as much of the old paint off as possible.

After all of the loose material is removed, pressure wash the entire floor with clean water to make sure that all the residue is removed. Areas with grease and other contaminants should be scrubbed with a solution of trisodium phosphate (TSP) and water and rinsed thoroughly. After the surface is dry, you're ready to paint or put down tile.

Acid Etching

If you have a really old and dirty floor, sweep the floor one final time and make sure you've removed all the dust. Next, dampen the floor and apply a 1:1 solution of muriatic acid and water. The acid should bubble vigorously when applied to the concrete. Coverage should be about 1 gallon of solution per 100 square feet.

Allow the reaction between the acid solution and the concrete to occur for three to five minutes, and then follow with a stiff broom. Rinse the etched surface with clean water, preferably with a high-pressure washer. Do this a minimum of three times to ensure a complete rinse. Whatever you do, don't let the acid dry out on the floor.

Household ammonia can be added to the rinse to help neutralize the acid. If you're really fanatical, you can use litmus paper to check the pH of the rinse water. If the rinse water is not pH neutral (pH 7-8) or if there appears to be a film on the floor, keep rinsing. Allow the surface to completely dry and vacuum it to remove fine particles loosened by the acid etch.

Flooring may be the biggest decision you can make about your new garage. This is what people will see every day, walk on every day, and this is what you will have to keep clean every single day. These are the two biggest issues about your garage floor—appearance and maintenance.

You're going to spend more money on your floor than any other item in the garage. The labor involved is equally intensive. You need to carefully consider all your options. Read everything you can find about the subject of flooring. Then go look at floors. You need to become obsessed with floors. Then, and only then, will you be ready to install your own garage flooring.

RESOURCES

Mid America Motorworks
Mid America Direct, Inc.
#1 Mid America Place
Effingham, Illinois 62401
800-500-8388
www.madvet.com
Mid America Motorworks recently added an extensive line of items for your garage. Since this is a rapidly expanding company it pays to check out their latest catalog and their website.

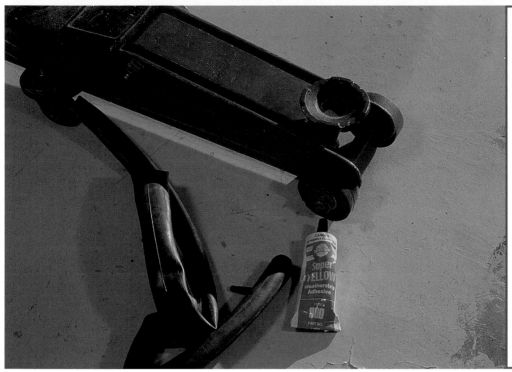

Floor jacks do a tremendous amount of damage to floor coverings. Fasten pieces of old bicycle inner tube to the underside of the jack with adhesive cement to save your floor from damage.

Concrete Network

www.concretenetwork.com

This is a tremendous resource for anything concrete. This is one of the few places that has complete directions for polishing the concrete floor in your garage.

FloorBiz, Inc.

www.floorbiz.com

Here's a mega listing of all the floor companies in North America. There is no critical evaluation of the types of flooring that might interest you but it's a good place to start looking at a variety of floor coverings.

Armstrong Tile

Armstrong World Industries
2500 Columbia Ave.
Lancaster, Pennsylvania 17603
717-397-0611
www.armstrong.com

Armstrong manufactures residential and commercial floors, ceilings, and cabinets.

Kiwi Tile

28921 Arnold Drive, F-6
Sonoma, California 95476
800-998-5494
www.kiwitile.com

Kiwi Tile manufactures modular, interlocking, polypropylene floor tiles.

Tuff Floors

456 Wright Drive
St. Charles, Missouri 63301
866-987-9385
636-724-9385
www.tufffloors.com

Tuff Floors manufactures MotorMat racer-designed flooring.

Precision Epoxy Products

4279 Midway Drive
Douglasville, Georgia 30134
770-489-0340
www.precisionepoxy.com

These people provide most of the epoxy shop floors for the Nextel Cup race teams. They also have a nice selection of products that you can use in your home.

Resto Motive Laboratories, Inc.

P.O. Box 1235
Morristown, New Jersey 07962
800-457-6715
www.por15.com

Known for their POR-15 brand of rust-preventive coatings, this company also offers an extensive line of cleaning and degreasing products as well as garage floor coatings that dry to an almost-ceramic hardness.

It makes no difference who you are, what you drive, or where you live. Storage is the number one challenge you're going to face. We can talk about flooring and lighting forever but it all comes back to the storage issue. No matter how much effort you put into your garage, it's going to look like a mess unless you have a decent storage system.

We have three storage issues to address. The first storage problem is what to do with all your tools. Most of us are absolute tool addicts. We could really benefit from a 12-step tool program. "Hi, I'm Richard and I have a problem with tools."

Another challenge is what to do with all the parts that you've collected over the years. You probably have parts for a car that you sold ten years ago. You also have all those parts you purchased on eBay that weren't quite right. We won't talk about all those parts you couldn't even give away.

The third storage problem is what to do with a whole car. This may be the car you're working on, or more likely, it's the car you want to start working on next. This is the car you were going to restore last year, or last decade, but just haven't gotten around to yet.

The good part is that money will usually solve all of these storage issues. The bad part is that most of us don't have much of it. That leaves us with having to design a storage system that not only works, but won't cut into the kids' college tuition.

RESTORATION PARTS STORAGE

Let's talk about the restoration crowd first. Your parts storage system probably consists of cardboard boxes. If you're a really organized person, you may even use a Sharpie pen to label all the boxes. That's a good start. The problem is that eventually you have a mountain of boxes in the corner, or even the attic of the garage, collecting dirt.

But you also need to have enough storage for a whole car—a car that's in parts. It's amazing how much space a perfectly good car can take up when it's in separate pieces. We're talking about a major amount of storage once you get into a restoration project.

We're also talking about having to store parts for several years, maybe even a decade or so. This means that the part you take off the car today will need to be found a couple of years from now. You certainly don't want to end up going through several piles of boxes to find it.

The best solution is to use clear plastic storage boxes. And you should still label them. If you're like me, you'll have several cars apart at the same time; you'll be happy to have these boxes labeled for this reason. The boxes can be stored on your shelves and the lids keep the dirt out.

This is a clever arrangement that combines both cabinets and open storage. All of the items that you use on a regular basis can be placed on the pegboard. The items you only use occasionally can be stored away in the cabinets. The only question I have is how this owner manages to keep his workbench surface so neat. I would really like to have seen this area before it was cleaned for the photographs. Phil Berg

This is a great design. The roof was raised just over a foot to provide for more storage. Rather than create a typical attic, the end was left open to make it more of a loft. The window on the end of the loft provides natural light so you can actually see things. Now, the only challenge is to keep the area organized. Michael Stewart

Lowe's and Home Depot have a great selection of these plastic storage boxes. Make sure you get the stackable type. Also, when you take this shopping trip, make sure that you get enough of them. These big companies have a way of quickly discontinuing items. You can return to the very same store a month later and not be able to match what you already own.

The big advantage is that these plastic boxes seal much better than the old cardboard boxes you've been using. They can also be wiped down to create at least a semblance of cleanliness. There will be just as much dirt in the garage as before but at least now it won't get into the boxes.

You might want to consider heavy industrial shelving in your garage. You can usually find it at an auction for a reasonable price. Keep in mind that this stuff is big and heavy, but it really works and usually has provisions for flexibility. Here, you can see how easily the height of the workbench can be changed.

Some tools are just too big to be stored in a box. This 3/4-inch-drive torque wrench is used to tighten the center lock wheels on the Alex Job Racing Porsches. Not only is it huge but it gets used a lot so hanging it beside the workbench is an ideal solution.

Over the years, I've tried every socket organizer on the market. This is the first one I've been totally happy with. It doesn't collect dirt and can be easily moved over to your work area. It's now available at Sears for around $15, which doesn't sound too bad until you realize you need about six of them. The organizers are available in both standard and metric sizes, as well as the three most common drive sizes.

One of the big differences in toolboxes is the drawer slides. The cheaper Craftsman boxes use metal-on-metal slides. They work just fine and hold up extremely well. Snap-on uses ball bearing rollers in their drawer slides. The feel of pulling open a drawer with ball bearing rollers is almost sensual. I truly believe that Snap-on makes the finest toolboxes on the market, but they're expensive and I have other places to spend my money. Expensive toolboxes are wonderful, and they'll impress your friends, but they won't help you fix a car.

RACERS' STORAGE

Racers have a whole different set of storage issues. If I had to pick the number one storage problem with race cars, I'd say it's an issue of where to store all the tires. The real irony is that some of these tires are just flat worn out and will never see a track again. Nonetheless, we keep them around, and move them from location to location.

Then we get to the engines and transmissions that are around the garage—the ones you intend to rebuild next winter. These big items are best kept on some sort of mov-able cart or pallet that can be moved around easily. That way you might even be inspired to clean around them occasionally.

Racers also need to be concerned about temporary storage of body parts. There are parts of your car that you're going to remove in between races. In the last chapter, you'll see images of how Alex Job deals with this issue on his Porsche team. As soon as the cars are returned to the shop, body parts are placed on shelving and kept out of the way until they're ready to pack up for the next race.

Storing air lines is one of life's little joys. You want them out of the way, yet at the same time you want easy access to them. The Alex Job shop created these wonderful brackets out of aluminum stock.

The advantage of open shelving is that everything is just a reach away and it's nice to be able to see everything. The disadvantage is that everything becomes a place for dirt to collect. Most professional shops keep things in the open to increase productivity while home shops tend to use cabinets.

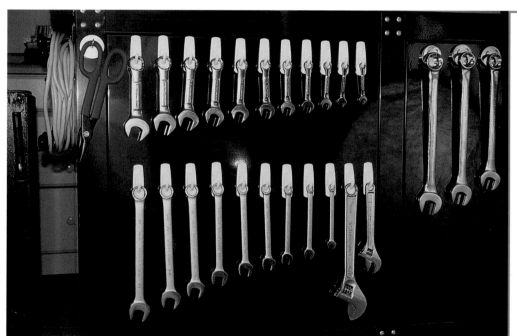

Wrenches can be stored in a toolbox, or they can be placed on hangers for easy access. Professional shops use toolboxes to organize their tools. The average professional has over $10,000 in tools and most shops are accessible by a huge variety of people. Lockable toolboxes are less important in your personal garage.

DETAILER STORAGE

This type of activity presents very few storage issues. You simply need a place to store a myriad of detailing supplies. The whole issue here is really one of cleanliness. Everything needs to be put away and the air in your garage needs to be filtered.

If I could ever seriously get into the concours thing I would purchase a portable room air filter. The filters circulate the air throughout the garage and remove not only the usual dust particles but pollen as well. Considering that

Zymol charges more money for waxes than Lowe's does for these filters, how can you go wrong?

You need to make an effort to combine both storage and portability with your system. If you are seriously into showing your car, you'll need to take a lot of supplies to the shows with you. You may even need to take some basic tools with you. This is why plastic storage boxes make a lot of sense.

Instead of packing and unpacking every time you attend a show, simply devise a system where you just load a few

Continued on page 36…

PROJECT 3 ★

Wheel Storage

Time: One day, or more

Tools: Drills, table saw, hole saw

Talent: ★★   **Tab:** $75

Tip: Measure everything at least three times before you drill or cut.

We really shouldn't need this. After all, the car has four wheels and a place for each and every one of these wheels. Nonetheless, we all seem to have a bunch of extra wheels in our garages. Worse yet, these highly prized wheels get randomly stacked around the garage because we can't figure out what to do with them.

When your wheel collection becomes sizable, the best thing to do is build a wheel rack. This is what race teams do to get the tires and wheels around the race track, and it'll work for our garages just as well.

Most of us are wheel addicts. We just can't pass up a bargain on that extra set of wheels. But what do you do with all the extra wheels floating around the garage? The solution is to build a custom wheel rack that puts everything out of the way but gives you easy access to the wheels should you one day decide to actually purchase tires for these wheels.

Make the rack wide enough to accommodate your widest wheels. If you're considering going to even larger wheels in the future, you might want to add an inch or two to the width. At the same time, you can arrange the wheels for height, leaving enough height between the shelves so that wheels can be easily removed. The rack shown here is made of pine 1x2s.

Keep in mind that wheels take up a lot less space than wheels that have tires mounted on them. In my case, I designed the wheel rack for wheels without tires. That saves me a lot of wall space and means that the rack doesn't have to be as strong.

I also needed a wheel rack that could hold three different-sized wheels. The rack had to be big enough to hold a 17-inch wheel and a 13-inch wheel. Is it possible I own too many wheels?

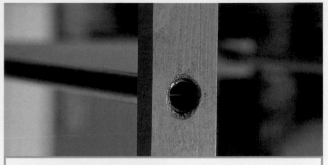

Drill holes into the ends of the unit to fit the conduit into. Next, drill 1/16-inch holes into the wood and through the metal conduit. Tap a small brad into the hole to keep the conduit from pulling out of the end of the unit.

Determining the location of the crossbraces is simply a matter of dividing the space on the end bracing so everything looks decent. This project is much easier with Simpson Strong-Ties, the metal braces that you can find at Lowe's or Home Depot. They make the project easy to assemble and they're stronger than any alternative method.

You need at least one of these center bars to hold the conduit together. The weight of the wheels will cause the conduit to bow out, dropping your wheels to the ground. The actual number of crossbraces will depend on the overall length of your wheel rack.

The horizontal members are electrical conduit that you can find at any home center. Conduit is strong and it's cheap. You need to decide how long this unit will be and which diameter of conduit you'll need. I used 3/4-inch conduit, but 1-inch would work just as well (although you should use 1x3 boards for the sides with 1-inch conduit).

This crossbrace is simply a 1x2 with properly spaced holes. I left it free to move so that it can slide back and forth depending on what wheels are on the shelf. Make sure that you install the crossbrace prior to assembling the ends for the unit.

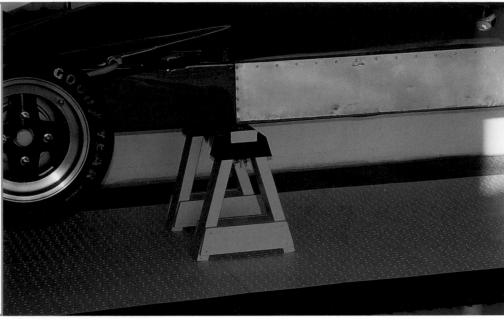

Working on cars involves a lot of bending over and getting yourself into some very uncomfortable positions. To ease the strain, bring the work up to your level. Jack stands can accomplish this, but a nicer solution is to place the car on sawhorses. You can purchase plastic tops for your sawhorses at the home improvement center and then use 2x4s for the legs and crossbars. I got really carried away and made mine extra strong and then I painted them with bright yellow enamel.

A lot of small tools come with their own little boxes. These are great for keeping things organized, but you'll eventually have so many tools it'll be hard to keep track of them all. You need to develop a storage system that works for you.

Continued from page 33…

boxes into the trailer. When you get home, you can work out of these same boxes and not have to unpack them. You might even have certain boxes for all your wheel cleaning supplies, one for the interior, and a second for the exterior of the car. That way, your storage system can be easily transferred from the garage to the trailer to the show field. At the very least, it looks better than a collection of cardboard boxes.

PLACES TO HIDE THINGS
Ceiling Storage

There are a number of commercial products on the market that attach to the ceiling joists and allow for storage above your cars and below your ceiling. These systems really create a horizontal storage space along the ceiling. All these years we've thought of storage as being vertical, but we've been missing out.

The disadvantage of ceiling storage is that you can only store flat objects in the ceiling. Remember, this is horizontal storage space. Seats are not something you want to store in a ceiling rack. On the other hand, it's a great place to store a hood.

Keep in mind that these systems still take up space and will restrict the type and location of your lighting system. I would put more priority into the lighting system than I would on the ceiling storage system. Design your lighting grid and then place ceiling storage units around that grid.

Shelves versus Cabinets

Here's where we have a real choice. It's also a question with no right answer. I've worked with both shelves and cabinets and there are advantages and drawbacks to each system.

Shelving is a lot easier to install. It's also a lot cheaper to install shelving than an array of wall cabinets. There are two problems, though. First, shelves collect a lot of dirt. All of the dirt circulating in your garage eventually ends up falling on your shelves. That means you have to clean them a little more than you might like. Second, no matter how hard you try to work with shelves, they always look a little messy.

The advantage of shelving is that everything is within reach and within view. Not much can hide with open shelving. This is especially true of the area directly above your primary workbench. When you need a spray can of cleaner or a bit of grease, it's easy to reach up and put your hand on it.

Metal adjustable shelves are wonderful since everything is in full view. Metal is also easier to wipe clean than wood. Griot's Garage

The advantage of cabinets is they look great. An array of cabinets hides all the clutter in your garage. When you close all the doors and wipe everything clean, your garage will look really organized. You can put everything away that you won't need on that particular day.

Years ago, most of us shopped in the kitchen cabinet section for garage cabinets, but it ended up looking like you installed kitchen cabinets in your garage. Several suppliers have now come to our rescue. Rubbermaid and Black & Decker have entered the garage storage market. Others are following these two into what could be a huge market.

We now have a wide range of choices. You can get everything from a faux diamond plate to a pure white cabinet. Materials range from pressed wood to vinyl. These manufactured cabinets come in a variety of sizes which should help you fill any sort of space in your garage. The biggest concern here is aesthetic. You want to select a system that fits in with your image. The Black & Decker cabinets are really inexpensive, but they also look cheap.

You want a unified look for your walls. Mixing and matching cabinets is not the best look. Before you install your first cabinet, decide what it is that you want in your garage. Next, decide what sort of surface you'll have. A very plain surface makes it easy to keep them clean. Never underestimate the amount of time you'll spend cleaning your garage.

Attic Storage

If you have an attic over your garage, you're truly blessed. Now all you have to do is make sure the rest of the family doesn't appropriate the space. You should have first rights to the space since this is space over your garage. The other members of the family can have access to the space over the living quarters.

The first issue is how to access this space. If your builder had any sense he installed a folding staircase in the garage. But these folding staircases cost over $100 so the builder most likely skipped it. You'll need to cut a hole in your garage ceiling, frame the opening, and install a folding staircase if you don't have one.

Keep in mind that the attic is best used for storing items you won't need for some time. Getting parts up and down the staircase is not much fun. Using an attic is a great way to get things out of the garage area.

The ceiling is a wonderful place to store things that aren't used often. This is one example of a variety of overhead bins on the market. Putting a lot of miscellaneous items in plastic boxes can solve not only the storage problem but the dirt problem as well. Put a list of the contents in an obvious, easy-to-read place on the container. You certainly don't want to get these boxes down very often just to remind yourself what you put in them. Griot's Garage.

Car Storage

There will be times when you want to store the whole car, but be forewarned. Storage does more damage to a car than any amount of driving might ever do. Nonetheless, we've all needed to get a car out of the way for a few months at a time.

Since each car is different, there's no single solution here. My Lola takes up very little space and is easily moved around. The Corvette, on the other hand, takes up a lot of space and is heavy.

Start by determining a location where the car can be as close to the walls as possible. The last thing you need is an immobile car in the middle of your garage. When you decide to store the car, don't kid yourself. The one month of storage will more than likely turn into a year.

The best storage technique I've seen is to put the car on four car dollies that allow you to move the car around the garage without starting it. You can always jack the car up on a floor jack and move it around that way, but that gets to be tiresome.

Things just go a lot smoother with the four wheels on dollies, but even with the dollies, you might need two or three people to help you push. I can move my Lola by myself, but the car only weighs 900 pounds. If you have a

Cadillac, you'll need four people. Remember, the job will go very quickly with the four-wheeled dollies and your friends will have more time to drink all your beer.

In addition to finding a good location, you should prepare the car for hibernation. Even if you only plan on storing the car for a few weeks or months, put it away as if it's going to be stored for a year. It may well be at least a year; things seem to work out that way.

RESOURCES

When it comes to storage, there's a lot to consider and a lot of money to be spent. Be careful and be informed. Considering that toolboxes and workbenches can cost more than you paid for your car, you need to be a well-informed consumer.

Garage Detailer
3057 E. Laurel St.
Mesa, Arizona 85214
866-364-3148
www.garage-detailer.com
This company carries the Gladiator line of toolboxes that are produced by the Whirlpool Corporation. These are midrange products designed for home use. The drawers use ball bearing slides. In addition to the toolboxes, they also carry the full Gladiator line of products.

Snap-on
2801 80th St.
P.O. Box 1410
Kenosha, Wisconsin 53141-1410
www.snapon.com
877-762-7661
This is the very top of the food chain. No one has ever questioned the quality of their products, but the price sends many people into shock.

Kobalt Tools
Lowe's Home Centers
P.O. Box 1111
North Wilkesboro, North Carolina 28656
800-445-6937
www.lowes.com
Lowe's has put a lot of effort into the Kobalt tool line. Prices seem to be roughly the same as Sears and the warranty is lifetime as well.

Craftsman
3333 Beverly Road
Hoffman Estates, Illinois 60179
1-800-377-7414
www.sears.com

This is a great solution to the problem of a narrow garage. If you place a shelf on each of these walls the garage will be really confined. With this cantilevered truss system, the Porsche owner has created a great area for enclosed storage, and at the same time allowed himself room to move about. Dennis Adler

This is the standard for toolboxes. No matter what brand of toolbox you're discussing, you'll inevitably compare it to a Craftsman toolbox. They make everything from the cheapest possible boxes to professional-grade boxes with ball bearings in the drawers.

Rubbermaid
1147 Akron Road
Wooster, Ohio 44691
888-895-2110
www.rubbermaid.com
www.rubbermaidcommercial.com
Look at what they refer to as Totes, Nest Boxes, and containers—a huge variety of things that will solve most any storage problem.

Griot's Garage
3500-A 20th Street E.
Tacoma, Washington 98424
800-345-5789
www.griotsgarage.com
You probably already get a dozen Griot's catalogs a year. They have a tremendous number of unique items, and everything they sell is expensive but high quality.

ClosetMaid
Ocala, Florida
800-874-0008
www.closetmaid.com
This company used to deal only with the living area of the home, but they've recently brought their expertise to the garage. They have a nice variety of things for heavy-duty storage, including some nice rafter storage systems.

CHAPTER 4
WORKBENCHES

I have workbench fantasies. I want my workbench to be more than just a place to put a bunch of junk. I want my workbench to make a statement about how refined I am and what a tremendous sense of aesthetics I have. This sickness comes from reading entirely too many issues of *Fine Woodworking* magazine.

There are three factors to consider when you think about a workbench. The most important is stability. Whatever else it needs to be, a workbench must be stable. Think about what you've done in the past few years. How many times has your workbench gotten wobbly? This is the number one problem with commercial workbenches that have legs made of stamped steel. A quality workbench has to be built like a bridge. This is going to be a platform for a lot of pounding over the years. After all, you're not going to pound on your nice floor. That leaves only the workbench.

The second criterion is functionality. Is the workbench really big enough? I generally find myself doing several things during the course of the week. This means I need a bench large enough to accommodate at least two projects at the same time.

Then we come to the all-important appearance. Does your workbench look like you follow the sales flyers in the Sunday paper? Alternatively, does it convey a sense of aesthetic appreciation and old-world charm? This is a highly subjective area, but one that's important to most of us.

WORKBENCHES

Do you even need a workbench? This sounds like a silly question until you think about how you use your workbench. In too many shops and home garages, the workbench simply becomes a shelf for miscellaneous parts. Go out to your garage and see if you need a workbench or just one huge shelf for a bunch of junk.

The first decision is whether to purchase a workbench or build your own. Actually, the real decision is whether to purchase a workbench that fits a standardized space, or whether to build a workbench that fits your exact needs.

What sort of relationship do you have with your workbench? Is your bench simply a utility item or do you regard it as something highly personal? A lot of people feel that a workbench is an extension of their own being. Woodworkers build a strong relationship with their benches. We gearheads usually build relationships with our cars, not our workbenches. Maybe that's why we put up with such lousy workbenches.

This arrangement is available from Griot's Garage. A preassembled workbench is wonderful if you don't want to create your own workbench. Keep in mind, though, that you're looking at over $1,000 of workbench here. While the drawer units are nice, the best feature is the 1 3/4-inch hardwood top. Griot's Garage

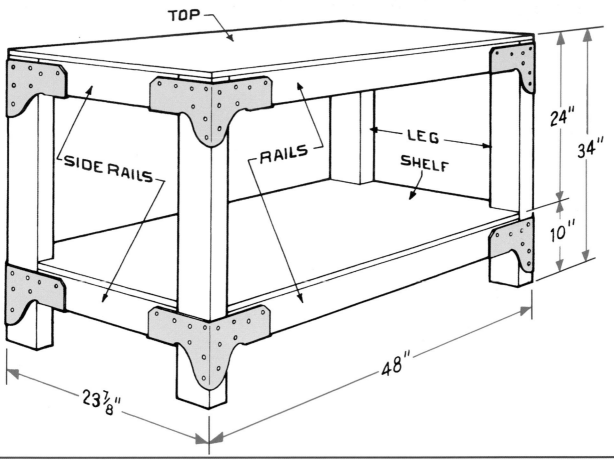

TOP
SIDE RAILS
RAILS
LEG
SHELF
24"
34"
10"
48"
23⅞"

Here's a workbench that you can build in a few hours, constructed out of 2x4s from your local supply house. Simpson Strong-Tie has created these marvelous galvanized metal brackets that allow just about anyone to create a solid workbench with no precision woodworking needed. You can create a workbench as basic or complex as you like. Consider building the workbench with oak stained lumber and powder-coated metal brackets. If you make the top out of two sheets of 3/4-inch plywood it'll be very solid and stand up to any abuse you create. Simpson Strong-Tie

Commercial versus Home Built

The easiest, and maybe the cheapest, way to have a workbench is to simply buy one. If all you need is a basic workbench, then going to the local home center is the least expensive way to do this. You can purchase a basic workbench for less than the price of the lumber needed to build your own. While a Lista tool bench, or even one from Griot's Garage, may seem expensive, oak and maple lumber will cost you even more, not to mention the cost of specialty woodworking tools.

The Wood Top

The key to any really good workbench is how solid it is. Commercial workbenches typically have a 3/4-inch top made of wood composite. That simply isn't good enough for most of us. The absolute minimum for a wooden worktop bench is 1 1/2 inches, and this thickness is easy to achieve. Take two layers of 3/4-inch pine boards from Home Depot and firmly attach them together.

You can overlap the seams and then epoxy the two layers together. Before the epoxy glue sets, screw the two layers together. This will give you everything you need at a reasonable price. If you wish, you can screw a 1/4-inch Masonite sheet to the completed top. This top sheet can then be replaced every few years.

The ultimate workbench has a 2-inch maple top. A high-quality maple top, about 8 feet long, can be delivered to your door for around $1,500. Making one will cost you almost as much, if not more. This is like having an old Mercedes in your garage. It's going to be big and obscenely heavy. However, every single day you use it, it will function and you'll marvel at the construction details of such a workbench.

Wooden tops absorb grease, which is generally not a good thing. Eventually, all of the things you move around on the bench will leave huge marks. After a few years, wooden workbench tops either attain a patina or they start looking nasty.

This is the advanced workbench for the truly obsessive. This workbench uses timber framing techniques—you're not only going to need some sophisticated woodworking skills, but also some pretty impressive tools to build this bench. If you go to all that trouble, you might as well construct it out of oak timber and then use an appropriate stain. Then you'll probably need to go out and purchase a 356 Porsche to place in front of the bench.

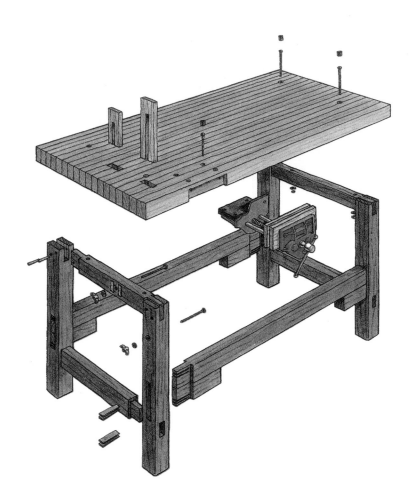

The Metal Top

Workbenches with metal tops have one huge advantage—they're easy to keep clean. When you finally put everything away at the end of the day and wipe down the top, it looks really great. It's even better if it's constructed out of stainless steel.

Over the years, I've used a variety of steel benches and reached several conclusions. A steel bench is great for working on carburetors. The cleanliness factor is phenomenal. The steel workbench top is ideal if you do much work with oily and greasy parts. They're easy to keep clean and with a little steel wool all of the blemishes go away.

On the other hand, metal workbenches have absolutely no character. They're simply hunks of metal positioned along a wall in your garage. They excel at function, do pretty well in terms of stability, but absolutely fail the aesthetic test.

However, I can't remember visiting a single professional race shop that used wooden workbenches. The closest I've seen to wood is the Penske shop in Reading where they covered metal tops with Masonite tops that could easily be replaced.

When you consider workbenches, don't compare apples and tangerines. Determine how much you can spend. Then determine what offers the best value in that price range. It's not always about what you like best. Think about which type of workbench will best meet your needs. Then try to determine which workbench will meet your budget.

Construction

Use large lumber when making your own workbench. Use hardwood somewhere in the neighborhood of a 4x4. For strength, use mortise and tenon joints, stretches to link the legs, and carriage or machine bolts instead of nails. A good workbench won't wobble or shift while you are working on its surface.

You can generally make a perfectly serviceable workbench with 2x4s from the local home center. Don't just make the legs from 2x4s. Give some consideration to bolting two lengths of 2x4s together with carriage bolts. This will give you the strength of 4x4 timbers without the expense. Very few of your friends and neighbors will know that you did it to save money. They'll just think you're very clever.

I love transparent plastic boxes for small parts. You can purchase a bunch of these for a reasonable price at your local home center.

TOOLBOXES AND CABINETS

Toolboxes are a big decision. Unfortunately, most of us started out with a very basic toolbox. Over time, we probably added several more small and inexpensive boxes to our collection. Now we have a number of small, cheap toolboxes scattered all around the garage.

A really good tool storage unit can cost thousands of dollars. That's why most of us have put off the purchase for so many years. The key to proper tool storage is to buy a total tool storage system and progressively add items as your budget allows and your needs dictate. This means

This is my favorite workbench top. A top like this gives you a stable work surface unsurpassed by any other.

your first serious toolbox purchase is very important. The brand you purchase will dictate the next few purchases. Purchase a cabinet from someone that offers a full array of accessories that will be available five and ten years down the road and match your original purchase.

You need a toolbox system that can be expanded so that as you acquire more tools you can add a middle section to the upper and lower boxes. You should also make sure that you can hang additional toolboxes off the side. You're looking for a toolbox system that can expand as your tools require and your budget allows.

The problem with the really cheap toolboxes is that most are made in China and the names change every few months. Even the sizes change, which means you can never build a total system.

The quality of the drawer system is key to a good tool storage system. There's no question that drawers gliding on ball bearings are superior to drawers that slide on metal rails. There is also no question that you'll pay extra for this feature. Both types of drawers will hold your tools perfectly well and both look nice with the drawers closed. It's all a matter of how much money you want to spend and how important smooth-opening drawers are to you.

I've used drawers with slides for years. If you keep them clean and don't overload the drawers, then everything is fine. Drawer problems usually come about when the big drawers at the bottom of the chest are overloaded with heavy items. If you're going to store some heavy equipment in your toolboxes, then you really should consider ball bearing drawers.

One very important consideration is the size of wheels. If you intend to move your main toolbox around the garage, 6-inch wheels are far better than 5-inch wheels. You

Continued on page 46...

PROJECT 4 ★

A Movable Workbench

Time: One day

Tools: Saws, drills

Talent: ★★★   **Tab:** Under $100 (not including the toolbox)

Tip: Use the toolbox to determine all the other dimensions.

One of the problems for most of us gearheads is that we aren't very good at woodworking. Here, I've managed to construct a workbench with a drawer system that doesn't require building drawers. I constructed a movable workbench around the middle section of a Craftsman toolbox.

It always helps to have the workbench close to your work. In NASCAR, they have huge war wagons that move from the transporter to the garage and finally to the pits on the day of the race. In your local shop, a low tool chest with a huge particleboard surface is very common. Neither of these is really that useful for the home garage; just make a portion of your workbench portable.

There are times when you want your workbench close to the actual work you're doing. For the average home garage, the commercial units are simply too large and too heavy. The large bottom units from Matco or Snap-on are also way too expensive for most of us.

Most of the time this workbench can be pushed back into place against the wall. When you need a workbench surface closer to your car, pull it out of the resting place and place it next to your car.

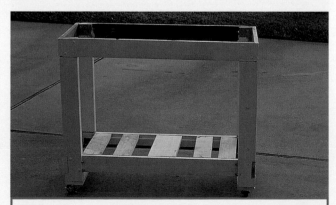

The first step is to create the basic framework. You'll notice that I've already placed this unit on wheels. The exact dimensions of the unit will depend on the size of the tool storage chest that's going to be placed in the center.

44

Next, determine where the shelf that holds the toolbox belongs. This will be determined by the height of the box you're using. You want the top edge of the chest at the same height as the lower edge of the top frame. A space below the tool chest can be used as an open shelf. I don't have to worry about perfectly fitting joints since the Simpson Strong-Ties more than make up for my lack of woodworking abilities.

Here the tool chest is installed on the shelf with a wooden bracket to hold it in place. This makes it easy to keep the chest in proper alignment along the front. You can even go a step further and bolt the chest directly to the shelf.

The only thing missing is the top of the workbench. You have a variety of options at this point. The choice is guided in large part by your sense of aesthetics. You want a work surface that's not only strong, but one that's easy to clean and looks good as well.

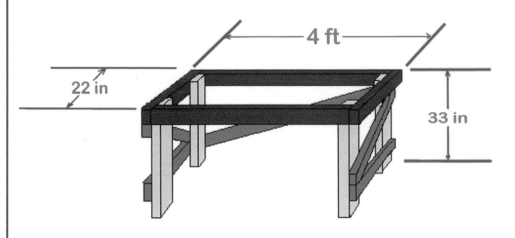

Here's the absolute minimum for a strong workbench. The best part is that it can be constructed with basic hand tools. The key is to use carriage bolts to assemble the bench. That gives the bench a lot more strength than if you use nails or screws.

22 in

4 ft

33 in

Continued from page 43...
might even consider a tool chest that allows you to grease the wheel bearings. But if you have a special spot for your tool chest and don't intend to move it, except for cleaning, then the wheels need not be a consideration.

If you intend to store heavy items in the toolbox, remove the drawer and look to see if there are stiffeners on the bottom. These additional braces can be very important if you intend to store heavy items. Also check to see how many layers of steel are used in the drawer construction. The expensive boxes are generally formed with two pieces of steel to provide additional rigidity. Also, if spot welds are used in the construction, they should be 3 to 4 inches apart. Anything less, and the manufacturer is skimping on the quality.

In the last decade, some toolboxes have taken on the dimensions of small homes, and they almost cost as much, too. When your toolbox has its own sound system and a closet for hanging clothes, you know you've gone over the top.

The lust for toolboxes can best be described as a quest for professional-grade equipment. You really don't need it, but you sure feel better if you have it. Take a second and look at what sort of toolboxes you *really* need. Then try to combine your needs with what you really want. Think of it as buying a summer home at the beach—on a much smaller scale.

RESOURCES

Fine Woodworking Magazine
The Taunton Press, Inc.
63 South Main St.
Newtown, Connecticut 06470
203-426-8171
www.taunton.com/finewoodworking
This is where you discover the ultimate in workbenches. The only problem is you have to build them yourself.

Diefenbach Benches
33498 E. U.S. Highway 50
Pueblo, Colorado 81006
800-322-3624
www.workbenches.com
This is where workbench envy begins. These are incredible workbenches from Germany. Prices begin at just under $1,000 and go to over $2,000—and that's before you add optional features such as doors and drawers. Most are over 7 feet long and at least 2 feet wide. Not a single one is designed for the automotive shop, but these are some incredible workbenches.

Simpson Strong-Tie
P.O. Box 10789
Pleasanton, California 94588
800-999-5099
www.strongtie.com
The connectors are a tremendous asset for anyone assembling workbenches and shelving units. They have a complete assortment of metal connectors that can make up for any deficiency you might have in carpentry skills. The best part is they give your projects incredible strength.

Griot's Garage
3500-A 20th Street E.
Tacoma, Washington 98424
800-345-5789
www.griotsgarage.com
Griot's has some basic workbenches for your garage, but they don't have the patina of an old German workbench or the high gloss of Snap-on professional toolboxes. You might think of these workbenches as the middle of the range. The good part is they're modular so you can arrange them to fit your garage.

WORKBENCHES

This is high-end cabinetry. Keep in mind, though, that units like this are still cheaper than the cabinetry your wife has in the kitchen. Cabinets like this allow you to put everything out of sight, making your garage look well organized—at least until someone opens a cabinet door. Mid America Motorworks

Freeww.com
www.freeww.com/workbenches.html
This is a great place to look for free plans if you want to build your own workbench. Some great workbenches can be built with basic woodworking tools and minimal skills.

L. K. Goodwin
890 Broad Street
Providence, Rhode Island 02907
800-343-2478
www.lkgoodwin.com
You might want to consider a heavy-duty modular workbench system for your garage. The L. K. Goodwin Co. is a nice place to start this search. They may seem expensive, but this is a lifetime purchase, and these benches are in another dimension from what you find at your local home center. These benches are huge, weigh as much as some compact cars, and last forever.

Concrete Countertops: Design, Form, and Finishes for the New Kitchen and Bath, Fu-Tung Cheng with Eric Olsen, The Taunton Press; $29.95
I fully intend to build a concrete top in my next shop. These first caught on in California kitchens and I see no reason why they can't be used in the home garage. Didn't you always want to be the first on your block with something?

The Workbench Book, Scott Landis, The Taunton Press; $25
This is another exercise in workbench envy. This book is actually a coffee table book about workbenches. The fact that it has a lot of good information is a value-added feature.

Build Your Own Custom Workbench: 13 Projects That Fit Your Needs, Mark Corke, F & W Publications, Inc.; $25.

CHAPTER 5
TOOLS AND OTHER FUN THINGS

There are tools and then there are big tools. In your garage, you'll need both. Hand tools are a never-ending journey. I don't think you can ever have enough of them. Every trip to Sears results in a few additions. Then for the true addicts, there's the Snap-on website.

The really big stuff is a little different. Items like an air compressor or a blasting cabinet are lifetime purchases. These are the items that are going to last you over 20 years. If you make the wrong decision, you're either going to have to live with the limitations or go back out and make another purchase.

THE AIR COMPRESSOR

I can't imagine working in a garage without an air compressor, but a gigantic unit is not always necessary. Most of us can get by with just enough air for filling tires and blowing the dust off our cars. In this case, you can purchase one of the little air compressors advertised in the catalogs and not spend too much money.

If you have a media blasting cabinet, though, you'll need a fairly large compressor to produce the required volume of air. Before making the purchase, be sure to think about future ways you might use an air compressor. Don't purchase things based on your current needs. It will end up being more expensive as the years pass and you're forced to upgrade to a larger unit.

No matter how large a compressor you purchase, make sure that it can be plugged into the normal 120-volt home electrical supply. Also give some serious

I placed the compressor under a small workbench and then used carpet remnants to line the walls. This keeps the sound down to a tolerable level and at the same time allows air to circulate around the electric motor and the compressor.

There is now a huge industry that sells lifts to the hobbyist market, but they can only be called lifts in the loosest sense of the term. The basic four-post lift sold to the hobbyist is usually nothing more than a storage device that lets you stack cars one above the other. A professional lift such as the one shown here is in another class altogether. This twin-post lift allows you total access to the undercarriage of the car. Michael Stewart

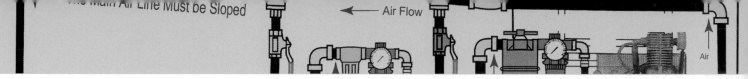

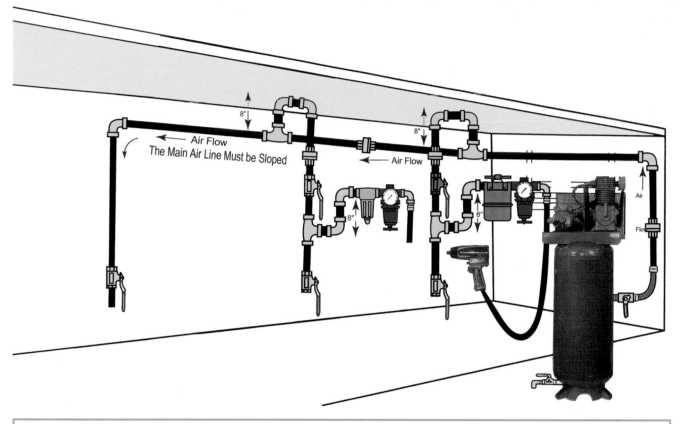

One goal of an air distribution system is to prevent moisture from getting to your air tools. The air coming off your compressor is always warmer than the temperature of the pipes, and this causes condensation and moisture in your air lines. If you install right angles in your steel air lines, most of the moisture will drop out of the air and can be trapped or removed through a drain valve. You also want the steel air lines to drop slightly as they go around the wall. Rather than installing the lines perfectly straight on the wall, let them slant toward the drain valve.

thought to the vertical models since they take up a lot less space on the floor of your garage. I'm really impressed with how small the footprint is on some on the larger units. The most valuable real estate in your garage is the floor. Anything you can do to free up floor space is good.

Air compressors make a lot of noise. If you live in the South, you can place the compressor outside and run some plumbing into the garage to eliminate the noise inside.

The loudest compressors on the market are the oil-less units. Before you even consider one of these units make sure you listen to it run. While the low maintenance is a wonderful feature, the noise is a far greater irritation than changing the oil in the compressor once a year would be.

If you must install the compressor inside your garage, you can place it inside a small structure that has soundproofing. A structure with cork or acoustic tiles can help the noise problem considerably; just be sure that the motor and compressor get adequate air for cooling. Compressors get very hot after running for an extended time.

The two things you need to be concerned about when you purchase a compressor are cfm (cubic feet per minute) and operating pressure. Every air tool has a cfm rating. You need to be concerned with how much cfm your air tools use. A 1/2-inch impact wrench only uses about 4 cfm at 90 psi. That's not a lot of air.

On the other hand, if you have a bead blaster in your garage then you'll need a lot of air. The average bead blasting cabinet uses 15 to 20 cfm at about 80 psi. That's a lot of air. If your compressor can't supply that much air, you'll have to stop every few minutes to let the pressure build up again.

Also pay attention to the pounds per square inch (psi) of pressure. This is how much air you can compress into your storage tank. The tighter you can pack the air into the tank the more air you'll have available for use. You'll have a lot more usable air at 175 psi than you would have at 135 psi.

When it comes to the size of the tank, bigger is better. A large tank stores more air, which in turn means your compressor will not stop and start quite so often. The

The Main Air Line Must be Sloped ← Air Flow Air

large vertical tanks that bolt to your shop floor are well worth considering.

Many stores give you a lot of meaningless information when you are shopping for a compressor. Sears, for instance, tells you the size of the tank but not the fact the compressor only goes to 125 psi. This means the compressor will turn on and off a lot to keep up with your use. Get a large enough unit that all of your needs are adequately met—the price difference really isn't that great.

Remember, cfm is about power and psi is about storage. If you don't think you'll ever own a bead blasting cabinet, then you can find some really inexpensive compressors. Otherwise, you'd need to spend at least $500 for a compressor good enough to run a blasting cabinet. Just keep in mind that a compressor that produces 18 cfm at 150 psi can be used for anything. Couple this with an 80-gallon tank and you can take on the world.

AIR LINES

I feel the same way about air lines as I do about extension cords—I hate them. They pick up all the dirt on the garage floor and become filthy every time you touch them. They are never quite long enough and always seem to be in the way.

Most of us start out with a neoprene hose connected directly to the air compressor. After a while, that gets to be a little bit of a hassle, and even more of a hassle if you have a blasting cabinet in your garage. If you're serious about your compressor, you'll want hard air lines all around your shop. A flexible air hose works well in a two-car garage, but it's a real source of aggravation in anything larger than a two-car garage.

The easiest solution is to run hard lines around the perimeter of your garage. Some folks like the retractable reels, but they aren't a total solution. Reels still have a single outlet and you have to pull the hose from one end of the shop to the other. Remember, you might have to fill the tires on the other cars in your garage.

With hard lines, you can place an outlet or coupler every few feet along the wall. Just treat the air system the very same way that you treat the electrical system—the more outlets you have, the more convenient it will be.

Like compressor tanks, the bigger the air lines the better. We want a huge volume of air coming out the end of the air line and only a larger line can provide that. When you run hard lines, use 1/2-inch lines—anything smaller is going to be a problem.

You also should use metal pipes to help remove moisture from your air lines. When the compressed and heated air strikes cold metal pipes it turns to a liquid, which is easy to remove from the lines.

Putting a lot of U-turns in the air lines also helps to minimize moisture in the lines. Water, being heavier than the air, has a hard time making all the turns. It gets trapped in the pipes and can be removed by opening drain valves you install in the lines.

THE BEAD BLASTING CABINET

I use this more than any other piece of equipment in the garage since there is always something that needs cleaning. There are really two issues that you have to confront. The first problem is the size of your air compressor—will it furnish enough air to let you handle your blasting needs? Since we've already discussed that, we can move on to the next issue. How big a cabinet do you really need?

TOOLS AND OTHER FUN THINGS

I'm not sure if you can ever have too many files in your toolbox. You'll never know which size you're going to need until you do a particular job. Always make sure you store these files so they don't rub up against each other. Purchase high-quality files—like most of the tools in your home garage, you'll probably never wear them out. Think of files as a lifetime purchase.

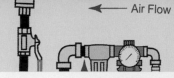
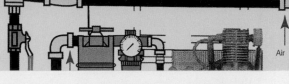

The Main Air Line Must be Sloped
← Air Flow

Air

PROJECT 5 ★

Air Lines for the Shop

Time: **Two days**

Tools: **Drill, large crescent wrench**

Talent: ★ ★   **Tab:** **$100–150**

Tip: **The most difficult part is aligning the outlets and having no leaks. Use a good thread sealant on each of the fittings.**

Running air lines around the perimeter of your garage is a two-weekend job. The first weekend, get about 60 feet of pipe from the local home center and a lot of couplers and fittings. You can either carefully calculate all this or you can just load your shopping basket and return what you don't use.

You'll spend the better part of a day assembling all this in your garage. Pre-fit everything and make sure it all works out the way you planned. Then take it all apart and paint it. The following weekend, you'll need a couple of hours for the final assembly. Once you have everything assembled, spray each connection with something like Windex to locate any leaks.

The key to this project is to have the air line slope downward from the point where the compressed air enters the plumbing system. As the moisture drops out of the air, it will run downhill to the end of the line. At the end of this line, you'll have installed a valve for draining the air.

The hardest part of the whole job is getting all the fittings matched up and assembled without leaking. I prefer liquid Teflon for the pipe thread connections. It seems to work slightly better than the tape.

I like to have an air dryer on my blasting cabinet. It's probably not necessary, but the expense is minimal, and this way I'm assured that the blasting media has minimal moisture content. I drain about a cup of water out of this dryer each month.

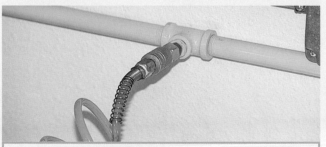

There are a couple of different styles for these couplers, so make sure that all the couplers in your garage match. I usually take an old one to the store with me just to make sure that I get the correct one. Space your outlets every 3 or 4 feet around the walls of your garage. The most difficult part of constructing air lines in your garage is painting the steel pipes. It's really not necessary, but it makes the garage look professional.

This is an air line dryer for the compressed air system. This particular one is installed between the flex hose from the compressor and the hard line attached to the wall. This setup removes as much moisture as possible from the compressed air before it gets into the distribution system. Don't forget, though, that as soon as the warm compressed air hits the cold steel pipes new moisture is created.

TOOLS AND OTHER FUN THINGS

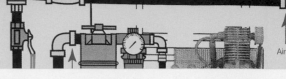

The Main Air Line Must be Sloped   ← Air Flow   Air

PROJECT 6 ★

Hose Reel Installation

Time: **One hour**

Tools: **Drill, cement anchors, open end wrenches**

Talent: **★★**   Tab: **$75**

Tip: **Make sure to attach the reel securely to the wall or workbench.**

TOOLS AND OTHER FUN THINGS

Retractable hose reels keep one more thing off your garage floor. How many times have you simply walked away at night and left your air hose on the floor? With a retractable reel you'll no longer have an excuse.

Ceiling mounts are ideal, but wall mounts are easier to install in a home garage. Keep in mind that the reel has to be connected to your compressor. If you install the reel in the attic of your garage, you'll have to run lines from your compressor to the attic. Also keep in mind that if anything goes wrong with your reel you'll spend a lot of time crawling around in the garage attic.

Prices run from $40 to several hundred, so you have to consider the various features. If you shop around, you can find bottom-end models that do just about everything.

Here are some basic guidelines for selecting a hose reel:

• Steel construction
• Contained main spring for safe, easy maintenance
• Four-direction roller guides to protect the hose
• Epoxy or powder-coat finish
• Ratchet lock for easy tension adjustment
• 50 feet of of 3/8-inch I.D. hose

Here is where the compressor line attaches; it's also the most likely place for a leak. Use teflon tape to seal the connection. You have two considerations in mounting the hose reel. First, you want the air hose reel in a location that's easy to use. More importantly, you need to minimize the amount of plumbing it takes to reach the hose reel with your compressor line.

These four nylon rollers protect the hose as you drag it around the shop. Even the cheapest reels have these rollers; don't even consider a reel without them.

This little apparatus allows you to decide how much hose you want left hanging out of your reel, which is especially important if you mount the reel in your garage attic.

These reels are heavy. Most will mount on the garage wall with four bolts. The concern is not pulling the reel off the wall, but rather the reel falling off the wall. If you mount it onto a concrete wall, use metal inserts and sizable lag bolts (these usually don't come with the reel).

If you mount the unit in your ceiling, you'll have to cut boards for mounting. The best aesthetic solution is to mount the whole reel in the attic and just let the hose hang down. Don't try mounting a hose reel to the ceiling. If the reel falls on your car, you'll have one very bad day; even worse, it might fall on your wife's car.

Use soap and water to check for leaks after you tighten the reel to your air supply. Teflon tape will help to create a good seal. When everything is connected and the air compressor is turned on, spray a little soap and water on the fitting to make sure it's properly tightened.

Always select a hose reel with a hose longer than you actually need. The hose will rewind easier and will be well protected. You don't want to start stretching the hose out and or pull the brackets out of the wall. Since the average garage is 20 feet deep, limit your considerations to hoses that are at least 30 feet long.

Larger is not necessarily better here since most of the time this blasting cabinet is simply going to take up space on your workbench. The largest item you'll place in the cabinet is probably going to be a wheel and that won't happen very often. Smaller units are more appropriate for most home garages as the bulk of your work will consist of nuts, bolts, and brackets. Think carefully about the space you have available in your garage.

Consider purchasing a floor-mounted unit. This choice means that you'll give up floor space rather than workbench space. Most people have more floor space available in their home garage than they have workbench space. The disadvantage of the floor units is that the height is predetermined for you. If you're shorter or taller than the average person, you need to consider this before you purchase a free-standing unit.

You'll also need to purchase a vacuum system. I used a blasting cabinet without a vacuum system and that resulted in a huge dust coating spread all over my entire garage. I do not recommend using a shop vac, although if you decide to do so, make sure you have a good, clean filter in the vacuum. The price of the blasting cabinet can best be thought of as a cover charge. Add in the cost of a decent air compressor and a vacuum system and the cost is not insignificant.

SPRAY PAINTING

I simply can't recommend spray painting for the home garage. I've painted cars in my home garage in the past, but it made a huge mess and that was before automotive paint became lethal. Today's paints require a special booth, an aspirator, and special breathing systems. These new paints are toxic and you really have no business using them around your home. Even if you don't care about yourself do you really want to poison your children?

Even using aerosol spray cans in your garage can make a mess. If you spray parts randomly in your garage you're going to have spray dust all over the place. It's amazing how far this dust can travel.

I was even more amazed that I covered all the coils in my air conditioning unit. You really don't want to cover your air conditioning coils in back epoxy paint. That's why I developed the spray booth described in the following project.

THE DRILL PRESS

The drill press is one of the most used items in the shop. My drill press is over 50 years old and is made out of cast iron. I love the old heavy drill presses. Any drill press you purchase should be a heavy-duty model. The cheap ones just don't have enough heft for precision drilling into heavy materials.

The main reasons you'll use a drill press as opposed to a hand drill are for precision or to make heavy-duty holes. In either case, you need to have a big, solid unit. The flimsy

Continued on page 58…

TOOLS AND OTHER FUN THINGS

PROJECT 7 ★

A Blasting Cabinet

Time: Three to four hours

Tools: Wrenches, rivet gun

Talent: ★★   **Tab:** $75–250

Tip: This is a case where smaller may be better. Think carefully about the size of the parts you may need to clean.

TOOLS AND OTHER FUN THINGS

If you read through the catalogs you'll start to believe that all you need is a $200 blasting cabinet and some compressed air. Nothing could be further from the truth. A blasting cabinet is really only part of a system. If you have a decent sized compressor you're halfway there. You'll only need a cabinet and a vacuum system to get rid of all the dust that forms inside the blasting cabinet.

The actual blasting cabinet should be the least of your concerns. Remember, the idea with media blasting is to send small particles smashing into whatever you're cleaning. Things actually get clean by being pummeled with sand, glass, walnut shells, etc.

Think about what size cabinet you really need and then downsize. The majority of the time, this blasting cabinet is going to do nothing but take up space on your workbench. We've all been impressed by the huge Snap-on blasting cabinets, but they're designed for a shop three times the size of your two-car garage.

You may think you want to sandblast the wheels on your car, but it's much more efficient to send them out to a commercial blaster. You'll probably only clean a set of wheels once every few years. The blasting cabinet will take up space every single day.

In addition to the cabinet, the vacuum system will take up precious space. The vacuum system is the part the cabinet the manufacturers forget to tell you about. Most of your time will be spent pulverizing the blasting media, essentially creating a sandstorm inside your cabinet.

This is a huge cabinet and not the best use of workbench space. I use it to strip and clean 17-inch wheels, but I only do that every couple of years. The rest of the time, I use this huge cabinet to prep fairly small parts.

The Main Air Line Must be Sloped ← Air Flow | Air

This smaller cabinet would be useful for almost everything you want to do in a home garage. The size of the cabinet has nothing to do with how well the parts are cleaned and prepped. The cabinet is simply a means to manage the dust storm as the blasting media smashes into your parts.

Worse yet, using compressed air to propel the blasting media actually pressurizes the cabinet, which in turn forces the dust into your garage.

The best solution is to hook a vacuum system up to your blasting cabinet. The vacuum system will minimize the pressure in the cabinet and remove the fine airborne particles. You need to check with the people, like Skat (www.tptools.com), who sell professional grade equipment for these items. The basic system runs about $250 and is essential.

The vacuum system removes the dust storm from inside the cabinet and filters the air. This Skat vacuum cost more than the cabinet. I tried using a shop vac for this purpose but ended up destroying a reasonably good shop vac with no effect on the dust I was generating.

TOOLS AND OTHER FUN THINGS

55

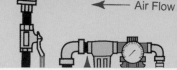
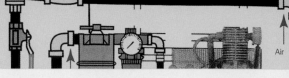

Air Flow

Air

PROJECT 8 ★★ *Spray Booth*

Time: Half a day

Tools: Saws, screwdrivers, drills

Talent: ★★   **Tab:** Under $50

Tip: The size of the filter will determine all of the dimensions.

A small paint-spray booth where you can use aerosol cans is one special feature you may want to consider for your ultimate garage. Remember, spraying paint or finish does produce vapors and airborne contaminants that can be dangerous.

The spray dust makes a huge mess on everything in your garage. It's amazing how far spray dust can travel in a garage. Before you know it everything is covered. This miniature spray booth will prevent that from happening. All of the spray dust is captured in the filter, which can be easily replaced with a trip to the home improvement store.

Always take proper precautions when working with paints, finishes, and solvents of any type. When it's not possible to take your work outside in the open air a spray booth may be a solution. Here's how to make one.

Build a box to hold the air filter, as well as the blower motor. The box should let the air flow through, but prevent paint and finishes from building up on the fan. A furnace filter installed inside the front keeps the paint from the motor. If this takes you more than 15 minutes to construct then you need to move on to another project. Make sure all the corners are exactly 90 degrees so the filter fits properly.

Construct this spray booth around the filter. The size of the filter you select will determine all your other dimensions. Here, I'm using a 20-inch by 20-inch filter from the local home center. Cut a frame that will hold both the filter and the fan.

This is the basic box with the filter installed. I cut some little brackets out of aluminum stock to hold the filter in place. I only need to remove these four brackets to replace the filter.

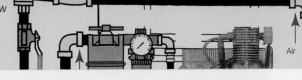

This fan is designed for use in a bathroom ventilation system. You only need a fan strong enough to create a gentle breeze that will pull air toward the filter. A fan that's too strong will create problems as you spray your small parts. Safety Note: Not all exhaust fans are safe for areas with flammable or explosive vapors. Make sure you select one that is designed for this type of use.

To complete the spray booth, attach PVC pipe to the sides using a flange and screws. Hang plastic curtains to form a contained area when the booth is in use. I use cheap plastic drop cloth that's available from any hardware store. When I'm done, I simply throw the plastic away and the area looks decent until I start my next spray paint project.

TOOLS AND OTHER FUN THINGS

Hammers come in a tremendous variety and you'll need most of them at one time or another. The only hammer you won't need is a ball peen hammer, but most of us already have several of those. We just don't know what they're good for.

Continued from page 53…

little drill presses may look nice, and the price is very attractive, but they will never meet your needs. If it's priced like a toy it probably is a toy.

There are several other things you need to be concerned about when you use a drill press. First, it needs to bolt down to your workbench. You want a solid and stable drill press for precision.

The next thing you'll need is a focused task light, maybe even a single track light that focuses on the item you'll be drilling. No matter how good your area lighting is, a focused task light will make all the difference in the world.

THE DRILL PRESS VISE

If you don't have a drill press vise then you need to get one. NEVER hold a part in your hand when you're using a drill press. Parts can easily be pulled out of your hand while the drill press is running. This can do serious damage to your body and it's not worth taking a chance. You don't necessarily need one of the expensive vises used for precision work. A basic drill press vise will be enough to keep you from getting hurt.

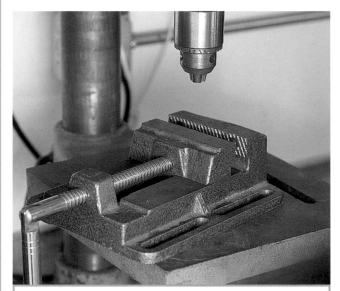

If you have a drill press, you need a drill press vise for holding things. A vise will hold parts securely for drilling. Trying to hold small parts in your hand is both foolish and dangerous. Drill press vises come in a variety of sizes and prices. Even an inexpensive vise will give you a huge improvement in precision, not to mention safety.

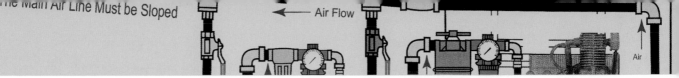

The Main Air Line Must be Sloped ← Air Flow

Air

Everyone owns several sets of hand wrenches. You'll need combination wrenches in both metric and standard, as well as box end sets and open end sets. That makes six different sets of wrenches—at least. Now the challenge is how to store all these wrenches so that you can actually find one when you need it.

WELDERS

There's welding and then there's sticking two pieces of metal together. Most of us really can't weld. There are a lot of times though when we need to stick two pieces of metal together. There are also times when we need to use a lot of heat. These two needs really require two different types of tools.

Very few people can weld with an oxyacetylene torch. There's just no call for it. In fact, if you don't already know how to weld with a gas torch, there aren't many people left who can even teach you the skill.

Skip the oxygen acetylene bottles and purchase a propane oxygen kit from Lowe's or Home Depot. You can use oxygen and propane or oxygen and MAPP[T] gas. These little units actually produce more heat than oxyacetylene torches and are great for times when you simply need heat for a project, and they take up very little space on the shelf.

Home centers also sell small electrical welders that are great for sticking metal together, but they aren't that great for real welding. Consider purchasing one of the more expensive units if you're serious about welding, but be aware that you'll need a substantial amount of practice to use one properly.

The cheap welders from companies like Harbor Freight are almost impossible to make good welds with. A friend of mine, who is an outstanding welder, finally just gave his away. He ended up with the Econotig AC/DC welder from Miller and is back to welding like a pro again.

When it comes to welding, you get what you pay for. A cheap welder will frustrate you to the point that you'll never learn to weld. If you plan on doing any aluminum welding you'll need a unit that can be switched from AC to DC. The AC output is for aluminum welding and DC output is for mild/stainless steel.

WORKBENCH GRINDING WHEEL

Another item that will get a lot of use in the shop is the grinding wheel. This is one case where smaller is usually better. If all you're doing is taking the sharp edge off a piece of metal then you don't need a lot of power.

You will, however, need a lot of space. Keep in mind that you'll often find yourself grinding a large piece of metal. Mount your bench grinder on a heavy cast-iron pedestal rather than mounting it on your workbench. This gives you a lot of space for moving a part around to get things done properly.

Take a minute and think about what happens if the grinding wheel pulls a part out of your hand. Where will this

A vacuum cleaner is essential for any shop. This is a handy version that mounts on the wall and is removable, although you have to figure out what do with the 30 feet of hose. When it comes to shop vacuums, there is a tradeoff between power and size. Most of the time, the vacuum cleaner simply takes up space in your garage. How much suction power do you need?

part go? Plan ahead and save yourself a lot of grief. The last thing you need is to have a part go flying through your car's windshield.

VACUUM SYSTEMS

Most of us have been using little portable shop vacs for years. The larger portable vacuums work, but they take up a lot of floor space. Luckily, the price of central vacuum systems has come down so much that they really are an option for your home garage.

There are a couple of options. If you already have a central vacuum system in your house, it's easy to tie your garage into the home system. The beauty of this system is that the hose is the only thing taking up space in your garage. The problem with a central vacuum system is you need a lot of this hose. If you get upset about long extension cords and air hoses, think about how you'll feel about 30 feet of vacuum hose.

Filtered or Non Filtered

Filtered systems use screen, cloth, foam, or paper to clean the air taken in by the vacuum. In any filtered system, the filters need to be cleaned and replaced. Most central vacuum systems are really designed for the living area of your home, not the garage.

How Much Power Do You Need?

According to CentralVacuum.com, homes of less than 5,000 square feet require a power unit of 20 amps or less. If you have a larger home, you'll need a more powerful unit.

If your home is over 5,000 square feet you probably have a four-car garage, and a lot of cash, so give the garage area its own central vac system. The garage is no place to start counting the pennies. Take a look around your kitchen and start adding up some significant money. Most likely your garage is the cheapest room in the house.

Bag or Canister Unit?

Decide whether you would like a bag or canister unit. Both systems are efficient. Would you rather dump and clean the canister or toss a replaceable bag into the garbage? Either way, you will dispose of debris less often than with traditional portable vacuums. I've found that you only need to empty a central vacuum system every six months or so.

An Alternative

If you don't have a central vacuum system in your home or don't want to install one, there is an intermediate step. Some companies make shop vacs that hang on the wall. For all practical purposes they're the same thing as a central vac system, and they're a lot cheaper.

However, they don't use the dust bins that allow you to sweep the floor right into the vacuum system. On the plus side, they're not as complex to install as a complete central vacuum system—you can hang a small unit on the wall of your garage in about ten minutes.

The biggest problem with the central vacuum is that you have to wrestle with about 40 feet of hose every time you want to vacuum something. My previous two-garage had a central vacuum system and I finally bought a cheapo shop vac to simply make my life easier.

PARTS CLEANING TANKS

I recently got rid of my parts cleaning tank from my home shop. After spending 20 years using a solvent tank, I just can't stand the smell anymore. If your garage is attached to your house, no matter how much care you take, you'll probably still be able to smell some of the solvent in the house.

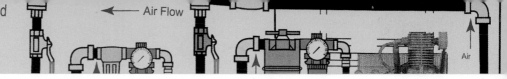

If you like the aromas of a professional shop you might enjoy the smell, but I guarantee that your wife and children won't. Even worse, the smell of solvent may permeate the interior of your other cars. If, or when, that happens, you'll be paying a heavy price.

The best way to clean parts is to use a large oil drain pan and brake cleaner in an aerosol spray can. This can be done outdoors. Brake cleaner works far better than any of the current solvents. Simply spray the part down with the aerosol, and then brush the residue off and give it a final rinse.

THE BIG VISE

Your garage wouldn't be a real shop without a huge vise. There are a few things you should look for in a vise. First, look for what is called a straight line pull. Next, look for a vise with an enclosed spindle screw. You also want a 360-degree swivel with what's known as a double lockdown. Finally, you want a vise with replaceable serrated jaw inserts and replaceable pipe jaws.

Some of the more expensive vises allow you to reverse the serrated jaws to get a smooth surface. This is nice but a set of replaceable jaws works just as well and is a lot faster.

If all of this sounds intimidating, keep in mind that you're going to spend several hundred dollars on this vise, but it's the only one you're ever going to purchase. Think of it as one vise in one lifetime. Most of the really great bench vises cost over $200, although you can get the same features in a smaller version for not much over $100.

The best quality bench vises are made from forged, not cast, steel. These are incredibly strong and will cost more than you paid for some of your cars. The ones at the discount stores are nice and will work for almost everything you want to do. The key word here is *almost*. Why not buy a really good vise and have one that will work for anything you might consider?

RESOURCES

Griot's Garage
3500-A 20th Street E.
Tacoma, Washington 98424
800-345-5789
www.griotsgarage.com

Craftsman
3333 Beverly Road
Hoffman Estates, Illinois 60179
1-800-377-7414
www.sears.com
This is the one we all know and love. They're the largest tool distributor in the world.

Snap-on
2801 80th St.
P.O. Box 1410
Kenosha, Wisconsin 53141-1410
www.snapon.com
877-762-7661
This is the very top of the food chain. No one has ever questioned the quality of their products, but the price sends many people into shock. The choice is yours to make.

Kobalt Tools
Lowe's Home Centers
P.O. Box 1111
North Wilkesboro, North Carolina 28656
800-445-6937
www.lowes.com
Lowe's has put a lot of effort into the Kobalt tool line. Prices seem to be roughly the same as Sears and the warranty is lifetime as well.

CHAPTER 6
THE ELECTRICAL GRID

You can never have too many outlets in your garage. You never know what you're going to purchase next, and you'll probably need a place to plug this new toy in, not to mention the light you'll need to see this new toy operate.

Actually, all of this goes back to what was pointed out in the first chapter—you need to plan for the unknown future. Who knows what's going to go on sale next? After all, if the kids can have a full array of audio equipment (that you don't even understand), why can't you have a few more toys in your garage? When you start to consid-er an improved electrical system for your garage, remember that you're going to have more tools in the future. Plan ahead.

In most cases, this means adding more outlets above your tool benches. That's why I like using wall-mounted junction boxes and steel conduit for running the wires around the garage. If you bury the electrical grid in the walls, you're going have a much more difficult time adding new outlets. It's almost impossible to anticipate all of your electrical needs right now. It's better to build some flexibility into your electrical system right from the beginning.

You want as many outlets as possible in your garage at an easy-to-reach height. Keep in mind that you won't be using all the outlets at the same time and the number of outlets in your garage makes no difference on the draw of electricity. The only reason your garage currently has one or two outlets is that the builder could save a few dollars.

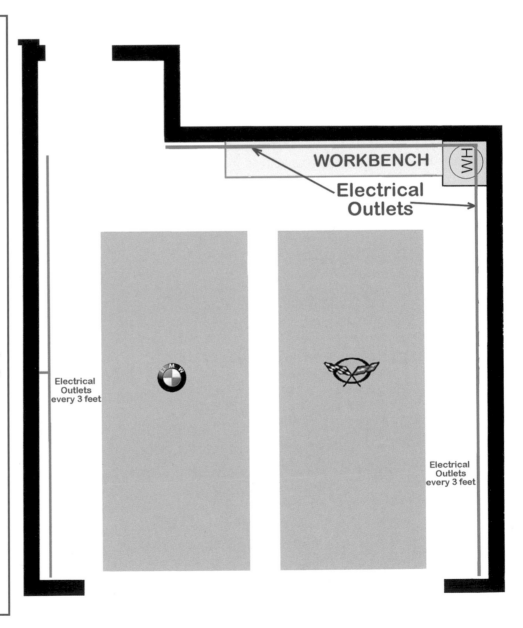

WORKBENCH

WH

Electrical Outlets

Electrical Outlets every 3 feet

Electrical Outlets every 3 feet

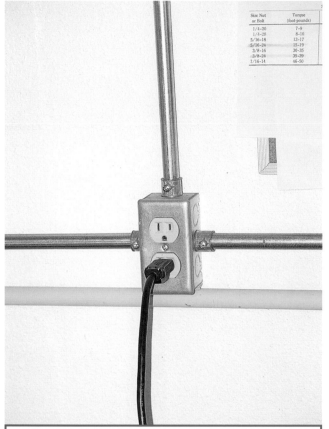

Size Nut or Bolt	Torque (foot-pounds)
1/4-20	7-9
1/4-28	8-10
5/16-18	13-17
5/16-24	15-19
3/8-16	30-35
3/8-24	35-39
7/16-14	46-50

If your garage is constructed of concrete, you most likely have the electrical junction boxes on the outside of the wall. You can simply extend the grid using conduit and additional boxes.

This is a plastic junction box that's designed to be used on a wooden stud. The face of the box is even with the wall surface. This is something to consider if your garage consists of bare framing studs.

This large junction box can be screwed directly to the wall so it is easy to use on concrete block walls. A large box like this is nice if you have a number of lines entering and exiting a junction box. Your electrical system is an evolving project. You might consider using these big boxes right from the start rather than adding them later.

THE ELECTRICAL CODE AND WHY IT'S IMPORTANT

Before you even get started, you need to be aware of the building codes in your area. Always consult the office of your local building inspector to determine what permits or special provisions must be met before you start to rewire your garage. Generally, any electrical work must pass local codes, no matter how small the job.

Be sure to get the proper permits, and be certain that you're clear on how to do the work so that it will pass code. Local codes may differ, so don't rely on the information outlined here. You can obtain a copy of local building codes from the Building Inspectors' Association in your state capital, the building inspector at your county courthouse, or your city's building department.

Some of the work in your garage may need to be done by a licensed electrical contractor. Inspectors usually aren't very happy with homeowners doing their own electrical work. The chances for electrocution or a house fire from faulty wiring are high, so inspectors check electrical work very carefully. Be sure all work is done neatly, to code, and

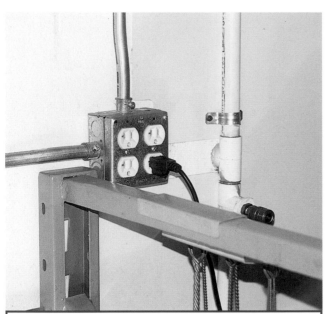

When you install an outlet box, you have a choice of either two plugs or four. On my visit to the Alex Job Porsche shop, I noticed that they use these four-outlet boxes at every location. The extra cost is minimal and there may come a time when you need to plug in more than two items at once.

Here's where it all begins—the main junction box is the key to this whole electrical grid. Hopefully, when you look in your box you'll find at least three blank spaces where new circuit breakers can be installed.

in the manner inspectors are used to seeing it done.

You may also need to check your community association rules. A lot of the newer gated, or deed-restricted, communities require all work to be done by a licensed electrician. This is something you may not have noticed when you purchased the home. Check the rules for your community association before you get started.

Also consider your insurance policy. If your wiring causes the house to burn down, will your insurance company pay on the policy? This may sound a little crazy right now, but it could become a big issue later on.

The issue may even surface if you attempt to sell the house. Nearly everyone hires home inspectors before they purchase a home. These inspectors are just looking for things to fault in an attempt to justify their fees. A garage that is not wired to code would be like a free lunch for them. Your garage could easily become a negotiating point in an attempt to reduce the selling price of your home.

The solution is easy—have your plans looked at by a licensed electrician. You can then install all of the junction boxes and conduit. Have a professional electrician come in to simply connect the wires. That way you're covered, and at the same time, you get the fun of doing the work.

IT ALL STARTS AT THE BOX

The first thing you have to determine is how much power is actually coming into your garage. The people who origi-

nally designed your garage had no idea that you were going to build an industrial facility in your home. They thought a person would at best need a couple of lights and maybe a place to recharge the leaf blower.

Now you have a garage with welders and air compressors, not to mention a dedicated climate control system. You really need to start right where the electricity first enters your garage. Even if your house was built recently, no one imagined how much electricity you might need to play with your cars.

First, look at the circuit box that distributes the electricity around your home. Do you see some blank plates? If you do, you're having a good day. If there's room to put in three or four new circuits, you're having a very good day.

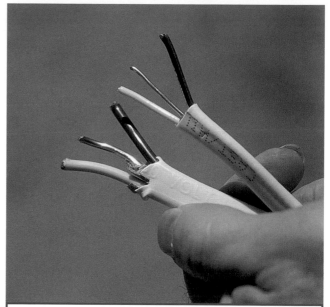

It's a substantial increase in thickness when you jump from a 14-gauge wire to a 12-gauge. The 12-gauge wire is also more difficult to feed through the conduit system and more difficult to connect to the switches. Check with a local electrician to see what your local code requires; there is no reason to use 12-gauge wire for most things in your garage's electrical system.

This is one way to deal with extension cord clutter. You want to be able to reach both cars with this extension cord so location is critical. Get the reel where you want it, and then install an electrical outlet in that location. You could also install the reel where you already have an outlet, but that never seems very satisfactory. Since you're going to live with this for the next decade or so you might as well take the extra hour and do it right.

If the box is full, you need to start asking around for the name of a good electrician who doesn't mind working on small jobs. You're going to need a new sub-panel installed just for the garage. That's not a big deal, just one more item that has to be done before you have your gearhead garage.

A sub-panel will give you a lot more flexibility to add circuits in the future and it's a good idea to install one right from the beginning. This simply builds more flexibility into the system from the very first day.

WHAT'S A CIRCUIT?

An electrical circuit is a road for electricity. Just like a road you would drive on, you don't want it to get too crowded. You need to consider what sorts of cars, or in our case tools, are going to use this road.

Electricity travels from its home (the large breaker box) to the electrical tools and lights in your garage through copper wire. Once it feeds the tool with power, the electricity passes back to the breaker box along another copper wire. When something is running, the electricity (or at least most of it) makes a round trip. That's why we call it a circuit.

Electricity can only move when a circuit is complete, or when a light or tool is in use. If this circuit is broken, the electrical flow stops and the tool stops working. The on/off switch on your tools generally controls the flow of electricity in your garage.

If the road is too busy, meaning you're trying to use too many tools on one circuit, the circuit breaker will shut the road down. This could also happen because the electricity is being sent to the wrong exit, or what is commonly known as a short. If your circuits keep shutting down, you'll need to do some investigating to find out why this is happening.

The first thing to determine is how many circuits, or electrical roads, you need in your garage. The more roads you have, the smaller the chance of things getting overcrowded. We'll get back to this point later in the chapter.

CIRCUIT BREAKERS

A circuit breaker is a device that will sacrifice itself to protect you from your mistakes. Circuit breakers shut your electricity off if you overload a circuit. If you keep blowing

THE ELECTRICAL GRID

65

PROJECT 9 ★

Time: One or two days

Tools: Drills, wire cutters, screw drivers

Talent: ★★   **Tab:** $50–150

Tip: Get a continuity checker from your local home supply outlet. They're under $10 and allow you to check that you've connected the wires properly.

THE ELECTRICAL GRID

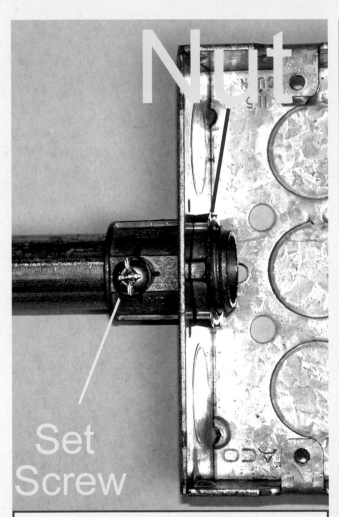

There are a variety of couplers available for connecting the metal conduit to the junction box. Look for one that seems to meet your needs and then standardize it throughout the garage. This type is nice because it allows you a little play in the length of the conduit. As long as you cut the pipe within 1/4 inch of the necessary length, it will cover up any mistakes.

I love steel conduit for garages. First, I love having all the electrical wiring on the outside of the wall. It's easy to make changes as things go along and as I acquire more tools and rearrange my garage. I also like the industrial look for a garage. I'm not trying to turn my garage into a family room. It's a shop and it should look like a shop.

Steel conduit is much safer than having exposed wires. If you start moving things around in the garage, there's always a possibility that something could bang into your wiring system and cut the wire. If your wires are encased in conduit there's no chance of that happening.

You can also use plastic conduit for your wiring. It's a little lighter and maybe a little easier to paint. Moreover, use some creativity with your garage. There's no reason for everything to simply be varying shades of gray.

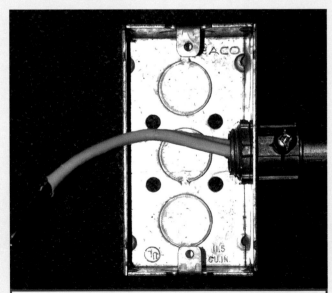

You want at least 6 inches of extra wire because you can always make wire shorter. If you cut it too short you may very well have 6 feet of useless wire.

the circuit breakers in your garage, you probably have too much equipment on one line.

Overloaded circuits occur when too much power is running through an electrical wire. To protect the wire, the circuit breaker detects the overload and turns the circuit off. The solution to this problem is to remove some of the things that are connected to the overloaded wires. If you really need to run all these things simultaneously, you should add another set of wires, or a circuit, to bring power to these tools.

HOW MANY CIRCUITS SHOULD I HAVE?

As with any other kind of home wiring, you need enough power for all the tools that will be running at the same time. The basic rule is that you should stay under 80 percent of the nominal capacity of the circuit. For typical home shop use, this means a circuit for each major power tool (such as a compressor or welder), and another one for the smaller shop tools like the drill press, bench grinders, and shop vac.

Lights should always be on a circuit of their own and not shared with any circuits. You want to avoid a situation where a tool is still spinning at several thousand rpm while you're groping around in the dark.

After years of fighting the laws of electricity, I've learned that the compressor needs its very own circuit. A decent-sized air compressor will need a 20-amp circuit. Even if you don't have an air compressor in your garage right now, plan for one—a big one. It's going to be a lot easier to run a circuit to a nonexistent air compressor than it will be to put in the wiring later on.

The compressor should also have a separate circuit if you use a blasting cabinet. When you're doing bead blasting, you use more than just the compressor. You also have the lights running inside the cabinet and the vacuum system running to keep the dust down. This means that you're probably over the limits of a 15-amp circuit, especially every time the compressor starts up.

Use at least 12-gauge wire in the compressor circuit since these motors begin with a big start-up surge. If you use a 20-amp breaker, keep in mind that many municipal codes require that you also use 20A receptacles on that circuit.

Install a separate circuit for all the other shop equipment such as the drill press and the bench grinder. None of these take a lot of electricity, but if you wire them on the same circuit as the lighting system, you could find yourself in the dark with some pretty impressive tools still rotating. You can also use this circuit for the outlets that run around the wall of your garage.

The area lights can go on the third circuit in the garage. You can probably put all of your task lights on this circuit as well. A normal 15-amp circuit should easily take care of all your needs here.

Line up the setscrews by leaving everything loose. Before you start connecting the wires, tighten the locknut shown in the previous picture.

This is the inside of the main electrical box before anything has been connected. You generally have 220 amps coming into this box. If you have an older home you may have less. Generally, 220-amp electrical service is just fine for everything you want to do in your home.

If you intend to use a welder in your garage, make provisions for a fourth circuit. This can be simply making sure that you have extra space in your main box, or you might even run conduit from the box to an appropriate point in the garage. Just remember that your welder may very well need a 220 circuit and a special plug at the outlet.

ELECTRICAL OUTLETS

You can never have too many outlets in a shop or garage. Extension cords are an invention of the devil. I really hate walking around the garage tripping over extension cords. They get dirty and they're always in the way.

The more wall outlets you have, the fewer extension cords you'll need. Anything that can reduce garage clutter is a good thing. Don't use extension cords if you can help it.

An extension cord is never as safe as a straight length of wire of the same gauge. In addition, the insulation of an extension cord won't withstand as much heat, and heat dissipation is the critical issue with electricity. When you look at your electrical system, try to hard-wire as much as possible and keep extension cord use to an absolute minimum.

If you install enough outlets, you can reduce the clutter to one extension cord. A nice 10-foot extension cord should take care of all your needs in the garage. Just imagine how nice it will be to not have to put that 50-foot cord away every night. If you must use extension cords, you should consider self-winding cords that automatically retract into their housings with a simple tug. The Eastwood Company offers a hand-crank rewinder for under $30 called the WonderWinder Electrical Cord Organizer that coils the extension cord neatly into a mesh basket. This unit is swivel-mounted so it can be used in a 180-degree arc.

Remember, most electrical codes require all electrical outlets to be at least 18 inches from the floor. Actually, I would go even higher so I don't have to bend down as much. Four feet seems to be about the right height for most people.

WHAT SIZE WIRE SHOULD I USE?

You could go through a lot of calculations, but most likely your local code already dictates what you should use. There are some basic rules that make your life easier.

For a 20-amp circuit, use 12-gauge wire. For a 15-amp circuit, you can generally use 14-gauge wire. For a long run, though, something over 100 feet, you should use the next larger size wire to avoid voltage drops. This might only be necessary if you have a four- or five-car garage. The 12-gauge is only slightly more expensive than 14-gauge, but it's a lot stiffer and harder to work with.

Here's a quick table for normal situations. Go up a size for more than 100-foot runs and when the cable is in conduit or grouped with other wires in a place where they can't dissipate heat easily: You can generally use 14-gauge for most of your garage work.

You might consider putting the air compressor on a 10-gauge line if it's a large one. That may be more wire than needed but it doesn't hurt anything. The only reason you would need something like a 6- or 8-gauge wire is if you have a monster welder. In that case, it should also be on a separate circuit.

Wire Size	Rating	Breaker Size
14-gauge	15 amps	15 amps
12-gauge	20 amps	20 amps
10-gauge	30 amps	30 amps
8-gauge	45 amps	40 amps
6-gauge	65 amps	60 amps

By this time, your planning should be complete. This is the actual garage outlined in an earlier drawing.

This line is run directly up the wall to a convenient location. I can add more outlets by simply running conduit parallel to the floor, extended out from this box.

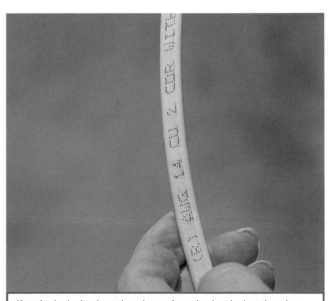

If you're in doubt about the wire you're using just look at the wire itself. All of the necessary information is written on the wire.

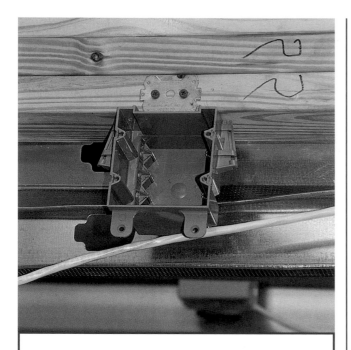

It's a lot easier to install junction boxes on wood framing than it is to install them in a block wall. Notice that we've routed the wire right past the junction box, leaving an appropriate amount of slack. After everything is in place, we can come back and make the necessary cut and connect the outlet or switch.

WHAT DOES THE "14-2" MEAN?

This cryptic number is used to describe the size and quantity of conductors in a cable. The first number specifies the gauge, or thickness, of the wire. The second number tells you how many current-carrying conductors are in the wire, but remember there's usually an extra ground wire in all the wire, and that ground wire isn't counted. Thus, "14-2" means 14-gauge with two insulated current-carrying wires, plus a bare ground wire.

COMMONLY USED WIRES AND THEIR USES

- **2-conductor, 14-gauge**
  Plugs, switches, lights (90% of your house wiring).
- **3-conductor, 14-gauge**
  3-way switches, split receptacles, etc.
- **2-conductor, 12-gauge**
  Selected heaters, air compressors, etc. (anything that uses a maximum of 20 amps).
- **2-conductor, 10-gauge**
  Any device that requires a maximum of 30 amps, which would be one giant air compressor.
- **2-conductor, 8-gauge**
  Maximum of 40 amps which you probably don't need in a home garage.

Electrical conduit comes in different diameters. The smaller diameter may look a little better on your garage walls, but the larger diameter will give you more flexibility if you decide to add more wiring later on.

Some communities require a minimum wire size of 12-gauge and do not allow the use of 14-gauge wire. Check with your local electrical authority to determine if this applies to your area.

WHAT DO THE COLORS MEAN?

Wiring is color-coded to make it easy for you to distinguish between the "hot," "neutral," and "ground" wires. These colors are standardized:
- Black or red for hot wires
- White for neutral wires
- Bare copper for ground wires

There are some significant differences between the neutral wire and the ground wire. The neutral, or white, wire is responsible for transporting electricity back to the breaker box, or source, after it's passed through a load, or the device using the electricity (such as a light, drill press, bench grinder, etc.). The ground, or the bare copper wire, protects the system.

WHAT'S A GFCI AND WHY SHOULD I HAVE ONE?

GFCI is short for ground-fault circuit-interrupter. Some people refer to them as GFI. This type of outlet is designed to prevent electrical shock and should be used in your garage. Most municipal electrical codes require that they be used in your garage.

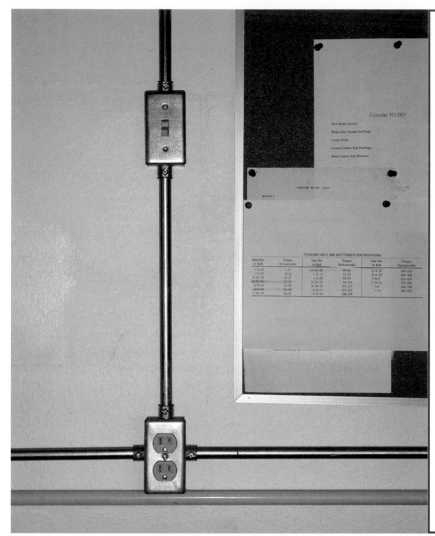

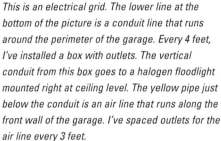

This is an electrical grid. The lower line at the bottom of the picture is a conduit line that runs around the perimeter of the garage. Every 4 feet, I've installed a box with outlets. The vertical conduit from this box goes to a halogen floodlight mounted right at ceiling level. The yellow pipe just below the conduit is an air line that runs along the front wall of the garage. I've spaced outlets for the air line every 3 feet.

Here's how it works: Say you're standing in front of the bathroom sink using a blow dryer and you drop the dryer in the sink, which is full of water. With a regular outlet, the dryer may just keep running, and if you touch the water (or any that has splashed out), you may get a bad—even fatal—shock.

With a GFCI outlet, the power will automatically turn off, thus saving you from serious injury or death. Now, if you have water in your garage, and who doesn't, you need them there as well as in your kitchen and bathroom. The cost difference is insignificant. At the most, it will add $100 to your total budget.

A GFCI outlet has two buttons—a test button and a reset button. To test the unit (which you should remember to do periodically), plug a drop light into the receptacle and turn it on. While it's lit, press the test button. The light should go out. Once you've ascertained that the GFCI is working correctly, unplug the light and press the reset button.

YOUR BATTERY CHARGER

Your battery charger will probably be one of the most used electrical items in your garage. You absolutely need an outlet, or outlets, near your cars so that you can use the battery charger easily. Most of the time you're going to leave the battery charger on the car for at least 12 hours since a trickle charge is best. This means your family has at least 12 hours to trip over any extension cords you string across the floor.

A lot of people use what is best called a battery tender for their collector cars. This is a battery charger that provides a very slow trickle charge to keep the battery at an optimum charge all the time. Battery tenders need to be plugged in all the time. Make sure you have an outlet near your car for this use. Leaving extension cords running across the floor for months at a time is one sure way to create trouble in the family.

This is a ground-fault circuit-interrupter (GFCI) outlet. Your local electrical code may require that you use them. These outlets are designed to prevent electrical shock and it's a good idea to install them at all of your locations in the garage. They cost a few dollars more than the cheapo outlets, which is why the building contractor only installed them where necessary. If you put them in every garage junction box it may only cost you a total of $30 more to be safe.

These buttons allow you to check the GFCI monthly to see if it's still working properly. Remember, you push in the black "test" button to kill power to that circuit. Then you restore power by pushing the red "reset" button.

RESOURCES

Electrical Online.com

www.electrical-online.com

This is a good basic resource for electricity. It has one of the best sections on permits and electrical codes. It also distributes an electronic newsletter about home wiring.

A SPECIAL CIRCUIT FOR YOUR WELDER

If you plan on using a welder in your garage, you'll need a separate circuit for it. The most common home welder is the red Lincoln "tombstone" welder. These units need 50 amps at 220 volts. That's more than anything else in your garage, and it means you need to have it on a totally separate line. If you don't own a welder but are considering buying one, you should wire this circuit in place.

The receptacle for a welder is unique. The plug on the welder is not the same as the plug on your clothes dryer receptacle—you must have a welder receptacle. This is one case where you might want a professional electrician to make sure everything is done correctly.

DoItYourself.com

www.doityourself.com/electric

This is a good site for the basics. It starts out with what tools you'll need and progresses through the more advanced items. This is one site that you'll want to keep on your favorites list.

LookSmart, Ltd.

www.findarticles.com

This is a good source of material about garage wiring. It's one of the few to point out the different code requirements between residential and garage wiring.

The Complete Guide to Home Wiring: A Comprehensive Manual, from Basic Repairs to Advanced Projects, Black & Decker Home Improvement Library, Creative Publishing international; $24.95
The Eastwood Company
263 Shoemaker Road
Pottstown, Pennsylvania 19464
800-345-1178
www.eastwoodcompany.com

WonderWinder Electrical Cord Organizer

Green Leaf, Inc.
11144 Toney Road
Fontanet, Indiana 47851
800-654-9808
www.grnleafinc.com

Wiring 1-2-3: Install, Upgrade, Repair, and Maintain Your Home's Electrical System, The Home Depot, Meredith Books; $24.95

Most people are very happy having a couple of fluorescent light boxes screwed to the ceiling of their garage. You're not most people. You want more—sometimes a lot more. You can never have too much light. You want it to be high noon inside your garage at any time of the day.

We have a variety of lighting needs in our garages, but they can be broken down into three categories: uniform light over the entire garage, localized lighting that focuses on an area within your garage, and very specific lighting for a given task.

Task lighting delivers light tailored for a specific task, including everything from track lighting that illuminates your workbench to the drop light you use under the hood of the car. The idea is to have the light focused on the particular job that you're working on. It's also nice to have it on a separate switch from the general lighting system.

The goal of your garage lighting system is to simulate the brilliance of outdoor light at noon. In the best garages,

it should really appear as if you're outside working in the driveway at noon. The secret to the dream garage is how close your light is to this natural light, especially if you're doing a lot of detailing work on your car.

Area lighting is critical if you do a lot of detailing work in your garage. How many times have you gotten your car all prepared for a show and when it's out on the open show field, you suddenly notice places where the wax wasn't totally removed?

On the other hand, if you're replacing your brake pads you need really great task lighting. You're going to have to check the caliper hardware for wear and that takes really good light that focuses on the specific area of the brakes.

You really can't have the dream garage unless you have perfect light. The good news is that a properly lit shop won't cost much more than one that's poorly lit. Quality lighting just takes a little more planning and about a dozen more fixtures.

This is the Robert Yates Nextel Cup shop in North Carolina. The floor area in the front of the picture is an epoxy surface plate. Notice the amount of light that's used in this shop. Precision Epoxy Products

This is one of the most creative lighting solutions I've seen in a shop. Petty Enterprises simply drops a fluorescent rectangle over the car, partially due to the high ceilings in the shop. The car is literally bathed in light. Precision Epoxy Products

GENERAL LIGHTING

The best place to start is with the big lights in your garage, generally, fluorescent ceiling lights. Unless you've been to Home Depot recently, your current lights are probably the most basic, and cheapest, lights that a builder could locate. Your home builder put in as few lights as possible in your garage, which works well for the average person. They're happy and the builder saved a few dollars. The problem is that gearheads aren't average. We need real light, and lots of it.

QUALITY OF LIGHT

Quality lighting involves both an aesthetic aspect and a quantitative aspect. The aesthetic aspect has to do with ensuring that your garage has a pleasing feel and ambiance. You can easily sum this up by how it feels to walk into your garage. If you and your friends feel great when you walk into the garage, then you have the aesthetic part down well. If you're blinded by glare, or you can't see the corner of the

garage very well, your aesthetic aspect needs some work.

The quantitative aspect involves making sure that there is adequate light for the task. In very basic terms, can you actually see what you're working on? For instance, if you're tapping threads into a part, can you actually see the threads? If you're adjusting the belts under the hood of the car, can you actually see the bolts that have to be loosened?

HOW BRIGHT IS YOUR LIGHT?

The most common way for manufacturers to rate brightness is to rate the bulbs in lumens. Lumens are a highly technical way of saying how bright the bulb is. The chart below gives a general idea about what sort of brightness you get from a variety of bulbs.

Lamp	Lumens
• 60-watt incandescent bulb	850
• 150-watt soft white incandescent	2,780
• 40-watt cool white fluorescent	3,050

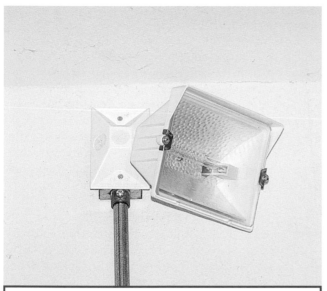

One solution for supplemental area lighting is to mount halogen floodlights at the top of the garage walls. This spreads an even layer of light across the garage. The glare can be very intense, though, so track lighting may be a better solution.

This is a standard fluorescent light fixture used by builders all over the United States. It's cheap and it's easy to install. There's no need to replace these fixtures since they work well with the proper fluorescent bulb and they put light out the side, which bathes the ceiling in light. Before you get carried away looking for alternatives, just replace the standard bulb with a pair of the Chroma bulbs. The difference will startle you.

WHAT COLOR IS YOUR LIGHT?

Bright is good but it's not enough. You also want a lighting system that accurately renders the colors of your fleet. You certainly don't want your red Porsche looking yellow in your garage. The Color Rendering Index (CRI) is a numerical system that rates the color rendering ability of fluorescent light compared with natural daylight, which has a CRI of 100. A bulb with a CRI of 91 shows colors more naturally than a bulb with a CRI of 62. Most standard "cool white" fluorescent bulbs range from 60 to 75 CRI.

The important factor is how colors look when illuminated by the light bulb. An incandescent bulb has all the colors of the rainbow; all colors of your car will be properly rendered if viewed under an incandescent light bulb. The CRI for incandescent lamps is a perfect 100. One of the worst lighting choices is a low-pressure sodium bulb, which emits a nearly pure yellow color.

Well-designed fluorescent bulbs have a CRI of 80, which is considered very good. The best you'll find with a fluorescent lighting system is about 85 CRI. That's well below the CRI of an incandescent bulb. Traditional fluorescent tubes are really pretty bad at color rendition. The standard incandescent light bulb is far better at producing high-quality colors.

Light Type	CRI
Incandescent Bulb	95
Normal Fluorescent Tube	75 – 85
Cool White Fluorescent Tube	62

COLOR TEMPERATURE

Now we get to the actual color of the light. Scientists define the color of light by its "color temperature." The color of sunlight is determined by how hot the surface of the sun is, and the fact that our eyes are designed to be most sensitive to the light from our own sun. Scientists have chosen to measure color temperature with units of Kelvin rather than Celsius or Fahrenheit, so the term appears a little strange at first.

A lower color temperature means a light appears "warmer." The common household light bulb has a color temperature of about 2,800 Kelvin. A cool white fluorescent bulb has a color temperature of 4,100 Kelvin.

Simply put, light bulbs with lower Kelvin temperatures (2,000–3,000 Kelvin) exhibit more light in the red/orange/yellow range. The higher Kelvin temperatures (greater than 5,000 Kelvin) will exhibit more blue light. Fluorescent (2,700 Kelvin), quartz halogen (2,800 Kelvin), and metal halide (4,000 Kelvin) lamps produce an impression of "white" light. Remember, if you're at the equator at noon, you'll have 5,000 Kelvin.

Think of the light in your garage and compare the bulbs in the ceiling to the sun that's outside. The sun is brighter than most lights, but it does give us a basic standard of comparison.

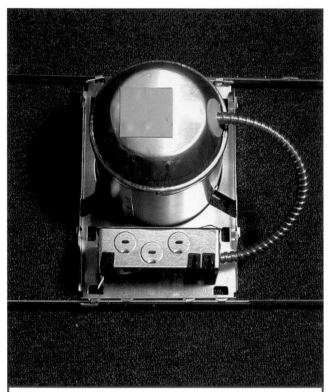

This is a fixture for recessed down lighting that fits between the ceiling joists in your garage. If you can get above the ceiling in your garage, you can make this fit and it's totally adjustable. The downside of recessed lighting is that you'll need about a dozen of these lights for a two-car garage.

Light Source	Temperature
Very Bright Sun	6,000 Kelvin
Average Daylight	5,000–5,500 Kelvin
Full Spectrum Fluorescent Lights	5,000 Kelvin
Ordinary Fluorescent Lights	2,700–3,000 Kelvin
Ordinary Light Bulb	2,800–3,500 Kelvin
Candle Light	1,000–1,800 Kelvin

NATURAL LIGHTING FOR YOUR GARAGE

Now let's sort all this out. We have natural light and we have artificial light. Our goal is to use lights in such a way as to make the inside of the garage look like daylight. High noon sun at the equator is considered to have CRI 100. The sunlight and sky light at the equator combine to produce a color temperature of roughly 5,200 Kelvin. A light which comes close to this is often called a full spectrum light. In order for a bulb to be considered full spectrum, it must have a CRI of 90-plus and a color temperature of 5,000-plus Kelvin.

Now what sort of area lighting comes closest to producing this type of light? It's certainly not the average fluorescent light bulb. Currently, the only fluorescent bulbs that come

close to replicating the light at the equator are some very expensive tubes from GE or Philips. These tubes (Chroma 75) will give you 7,500 Kelvin with a 95 CRI. That's pretty impressive. The Chroma 50 has a color temperature of around 5,000 Kelvin and a CRI of around 90—also pretty impressive. Both simulate the daylight/sunlight combination and both try to simulate a northern skylight. The lamps come in standard types—typically a 4-foot tube rated for 40 watts—and fit into lighting fixtures that are easily found in hardware and home center stores. They're also at least three times as expensive as the average fluorescent tube. So ask yourself, how much do you value your garage?

THE LIGHT FIXTURES

Bare fluorescent lights are rather poor from the standard of visual comfort. You don't want bare bulbs in your office, or your garage, which means buying a recessed fixture or one that screws into the ceiling to enclose your tubes. A recessed fixture looks really nice but cuts down on the amount of available light in your garage.

Fixtures that simply screw into the ceiling put light out of the sides, which bathes the ceiling in light. At the same time, they put as much light down on the floor as the recessed fixtures. Recessed fixtures may be more aesthetically pleasing but put a little less light into your garage. The choice is yours to make.

You may decide to install recessed incandescent light fixtures in the ceiling. Many of us have this type of fixture inside our houses. These lights are more expensive to install and more expensive to operate, but the quality of the light is superior to even the best fluorescent lights. These recessed lighting fixtures come in 4-, 5-, and 6-inch diameters. The 6-inch units really only work if you have ceilings over 10 feet in height. Generally, the 4-inch units are too close to being a task light and aren't a good choice for general area lighting. The 5-inch recessed lights are the standard of the industry for home lighting. They're really the best choice for your garage as well. You should space your lights 3 to 4 feet apart to get good overall coverage in your garage.

You should also determine where the ceiling joists are in your garage and place your lights accordingly. If you place a row of lights between the joists, you'll have less trouble running wire than if you place them between different joists. This makes the installation easier by minimizing the number of joists that you have to run wire through.

One final decision you should consider is whether you want the entire ceiling on one switch. With a two-car garage this really isn't much of a decision. But if you have two, three, or more bays then you might consider having several switches. If you do this, keep in mind that you'll be adding a few more circuits and making the wiring job just a little more difficult.

Portable halogen lights put out a tremendous amount of light; they also put out a lot of glare and heat. They're so cheap you might as well have one around your garage. I use mine a lot when the car is on jack stands and I need light under the car. Just move the light around so you don't burn yourself.

WORKBENCH LIGHTING

You may very well have workbench-type lighting in your kitchen above the countertops. Make sure that the actual source of the light is concealed from each viewing angle, no matter how severe. The actual workbench light source should really be invisible, just like in your kitchen.

There are four types of undercabinet lights commonly used: fluorescent, halogen strip, track, and puck lighting. You can use any of these lights mounted to the cabinets or shelf just above your workbench.

Halogen strips come in the same type of enclosure as fluorescent fixtures, but instead of a long tube, they have several small halogen bulbs. These fixtures look good, put off nice, bright light, and can be dimmed.

Halogen lamps produce light by heating a tungsten filament, the hot wire inside the lamp. Halogen filament lamps are less efficient than fluorescent, so for the same lighting level, it always costs more to use halogen lamps.

Halogen lights can be either plugged into an outlet or hard-wired into a transformer. I don't find either one to be totally satisfactory. Plugging the transformer into an outlet means that you lose an outlet you might need to use at some point. It also means you have one more cord to hide, or worse yet, let dangle. This can be eliminated if you hard-wire directly into your garage's electrical system, the only disadvantage being that you've created a semi-permanent lighting arrangement.

When you're trying to decide how far apart to mount the small halogen lights, measure the distance between the bottom of the shelf above your workbench and the workbench surface. Mount the lights the same number of inches from each other as the height they are from your workbench. Using this formula, you'll have a number of lights up under your shelving. You'll also have some pretty harsh light on your bench given the intensity of halogen lights.

Generally, I would advise you to stay away from halogen lights in your workbench area. The pinpoint nature of halogen lighting rules it out for most garage use. The intensity is nice, but it's so highly focused that it's distracting. Remember, you don't want to see the light; you want to see the part you're working on.

Track lights are not enclosed and they're wired to a transformer that lowers the voltage supplying the fixture to 12 volts. Track lighting can be placed both inside and below cabinets and can be controlled by a dimmer. These small tracks work great when the fixture needs to fit in a small place and not be seen.

Track lighting is primarily used in commercial applications. Most lighting experts only use track lighting for a very specific purpose. For example, there might not be enough room in the ceiling for recessed lights and you want to fully light the car you're detailing. You can also use track lighting when you want to illuminate a specific area of your shop like the drill press.

Continued on page 80...

PROJECT 10 ★

Time: One day

Tools: Wire cutters, drills, screwdrivers

Talent: ★★★   Tab: $50 or more, depending on how much distance you want to cover

Tip: Make sure you know what you're trying to illuminate with the track lights.

Get a cup of coffee and go out to the garage. Spend some time looking at your ceiling and decide on the best placement of the track sections. Plan for the first section to start at an existing ceiling junction box from which the new lighting can receive power. From there, you can carry the track along one side of the garage or around the entire perimeter of the garage. T- and L-shaped track connectors enable flexible layout and track branching.

As you think about the track locations, keep in mind that the fixtures can be adjusted in any direction giving you the ability to provide both general room illumination and task lighting from a single track. After you've determined the best track configuration, preassemble all the necessary track, connectors, and lighting fixtures on the floor of your garage. Do this before you start attaching things to the ceiling.

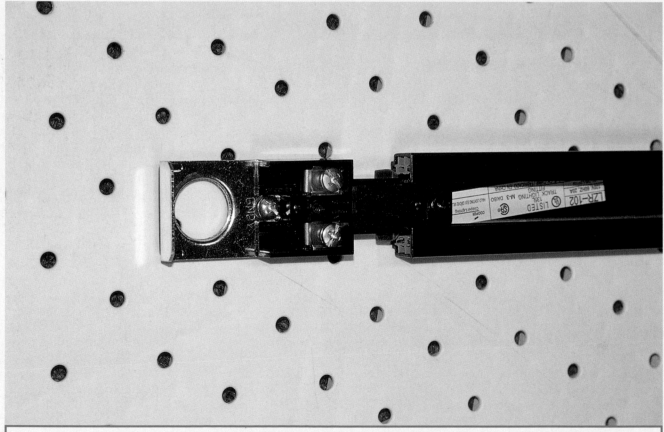

Slide the feed connector onto one end of the first track section and use the setscrew to lock the connector in place. Depending upon your layout, install either a T or adjustable L connector to the other end of the track. Use the T connector when you need to join three track sections. The L connector is adjustable to handle straight and angled joints between two tracks.

LET THERE BE LIGHT

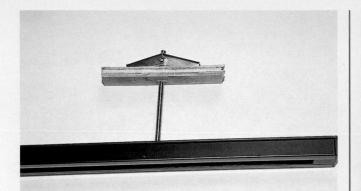

Each length of track is held to the ceiling with toggle bolt-type hollow-wall fasteners. If your garage doesn't have an attic, the toggle bolts require holes in the ceiling that are large enough for the expanding spring clips to pass through (usually ½ to ⅝ inch in diameter). To begin the process of securing the tracks to the ceiling, hold the first track section in place and mark the toggle bolt hole locations on the ceiling. Then, remove the track and use a drill to bore the holes for the bolts.

Install the toggles on the track section and push the spring-clip ends of the bolts through the holes. Since assembly of the entire track layout requires some flexibility in the system to make connections, let each piece hang loosely from its bolts until all the tracks are in place.

Now mark and drill the holes for the second length of track. Slide this second section onto the connector at the end of the first piece, and then feed the toggles through their holes in the ceiling. Tighten the setscrew that holds the track to the connector.

To install the first lamp, push the top of the fixture into the track with the contacts parallel to the length of the track. Rotate the fixture a quarter turn, so that its polarity arrow points toward the polarity line that appears on the track—you'll hear it click into place. Each fixture has a switch. After the lamps are in place, make sure that their switches are on.

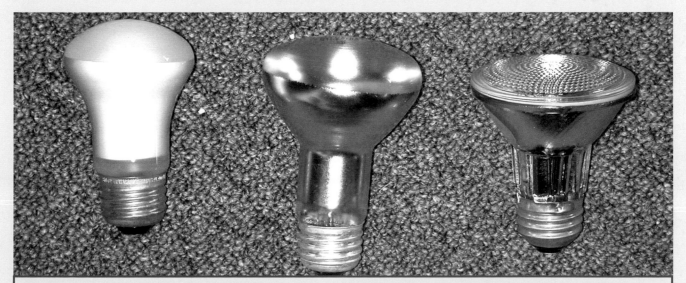

Who thought light bulb selection would be so hard? While the narrow floodlight provides the brightest light, it's more widely dispersed than the standard floodlight light. The narrow floodlight has a 30-degree dispersal pattern, and the floodlight has a 45-degree dispersal pattern. Just buy a couple of bulbs and see which one meets your need best; you might decide to have different types in different locations.

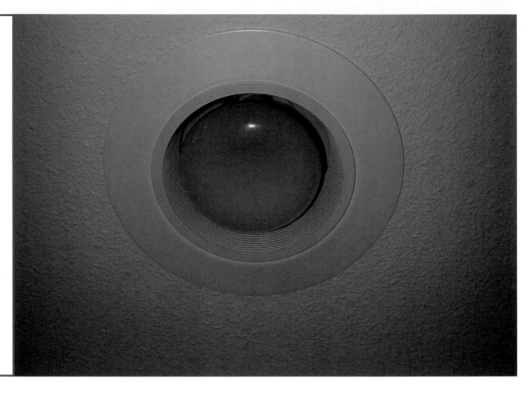

Recessed fixtures give your ceiling a clean look. They're attractive without giving your garage that dreaded rec room look, and if you install enough of them, you can have total coverage with a color-balanced light.

Continued from page 77…

Puck lights are small round lights with halogen bulbs. They fit in tight spots and can be controlled by a dimmer. Place several of them in a row under your cabinets and above your workbench. The distance you space them will depend on the distance between the surface of your workbench and the height of the bulb.

Xenon lights are fairly new to the garage. These are really halogen bulbs that use xenon instead of argon or krypton as the fill gas to improve the performance of the bulb. Xenon-halogen is a more precise description of these lights.

SHOULD I TURN MY LIGHTS OFF?

A lot of us have been led to believe that we should leave our fluorescent lights on since they take a surge of power to get going. That is true, but the surge is so small that it doesn't make any difference.

Turn regular light bulbs off anytime you're not using them. Turn fluorescent lights off if you're not going to use them within 15 minutes. Any extra power it takes to turn them back on is roughly equivalent to the power it takes to run them for 15 minutes. Turning on a fluorescent bulb is rough on the bulb. The more often you turn your lights on and off, the more often you'll have to replace them.

They're designed to work well in damp locations like kitchens and bathrooms. They give off little heat and run off a transformer at a low voltage.

Fluorescent lighting has been the standard undercounter light for years. It comes in a variety of sizes and can be easily installed under cabinets. It's probably still the best all-around lighting system for your workbench. Fluorescent fixtures are also the least expensive to purchase and the most economical to operate. Fluorescent fixtures can't be dimmed without using a special ballast, although for most of us that's really not a factor.

TRACK LIGHTING

Mounting height is critical for effective lighting, but how high you mount a light is a trade-off. If you mount a spotlight or floodlight low, it will shine in your eyes. Mounting a light on the ceiling makes it less likely that you'll get glare in your eyes. This is where track lighting excels.

Furthermore, you can aim the light at an angle. However, since light spreads out as it leaves the bulb, you'll need a brighter bulb the higher you mount a light.

Watch out for shadows around your workbench area with track lighting. You can really go wild with track lighting in your garage, and if it doesn't illuminate what you had in mind, you can just move the fixture a little farther down the line. It might not be a bad idea to run a track around the whole perimeter of your garage.

	Sylvania Mini-Floodlight	Sylvania Floodlight	Sylvania Halogen PAR 20
Lumens	235	420	550
Beam Spread	—	45	30
Energy Used	40	50	50
Hours of Life	1,500	2,000	2,500
Price	$2.97	$3.42	$7.48

WHAT'S A PAR LIGHT?

PAR stands for parabolic aluminized reflector and is a term applied to spotlights and floodlights used by homeowners and small businesses in track lighting. PAR fixtures are typically mounted on a movable track so you can aim the light where you need it. The PAR bulbs control light more precisely, which is why they make such great task lights. They produce about four times the light of regular bulbs and are used in recessed and track lighting.

Just to confuse the issue, these bulbs are sometimes referred to as spotlights or floodlights. Despite their different names, floodlights and spotlights aren't significantly different. A spotlight casts its light nearly as wide and far as a floodlight, even though the name might imply greater light control.

MOVABLE LIGHTING

Up to this point, I've dealt with lights that are either attached to the wall or the ceiling. Every home center is now filled with portable halogen lighting for a very reasonable price. These are wonderful lights with a couple of serious drawbacks.

The biggest problem with these lights is they give off a tremendous amount of heat. You really don't want these lights too close to you as you do your work. That's one reason so many of the lights come with their own stands. The idea is to get the light focused on your work, but at the same time placed far enough away so you don't burn yourself from the intense heat.

RESOURCES

Philips Lighting
www.lighting.philips.com
This is a mega site with more than you could ever want to know about lighting.

General Electric
800-GELIGHT
www.gelighting.com
This wonderful site lets you play with all sorts of lighting. It also has more information about lights than any sane person needs to know.

LIGHT BULB FACTS

Fact No. 1

The sun produces a continuous spectrum of light that spans infrared, visible, and ultraviolet light. What our eyes perceive as white sunlight is really a mixture of all the colors of the rainbow. Different light bulbs produce different colors. No light bulb produces the true white color that we see in sunlight.

Fact No. 2

Light bulb manufacturers design light bulbs by selecting a compromise between three factors: lumens, watts, and life (in hours). A light bulb can be designed to produce more light for the same watts, but it will have a much shorter life. Some long-life bulbs have lower brightness, with the company taking advantage of the fact that you can't see the difference. The same game can be played with bulbs that use less electricity—a 52-watt bulb uses less electricity than a 60-watt bulb, but your eyes can't see that one is dimmer than the other.

Fact No. 3

Light bulbs are sold by their wattage, not their lumens or efficiency. This is practical when comparing two light bulbs of the same technology. An incandescent bulb at 100 watts will produce more light than an incandescent bulb at 75 watts. The comparison doesn't work, though, when comparing two light bulbs of different technologies. A halogen bulb at 75 watts may produce as much light as an incandescent bulb at 100 watts.

Lighting Universe
888-404-2744
www.lightinguniverse.com
This is a wonderful place to look at lighting fixtures. It has a larger selection than you'll find at your local home improvement center, and a great selection of lights designed for commercial applications.

CHAPTER 8

CLIMATE CONTROL

Personal comfort is important. You're unlikely to spend much time, let alone do any productive work, in a garage that's uncomfortable. We've all worked in cold, wet garages. We've also worked in too many sweltering places. None of it was fun.

No matter how nice your floors might look and how bright your lighting system is, you won't spend much time in a garage that's below freezing. You won't spend much time in a garage where the temperature goes over 100 degrees either.

For that reason, it's important to include heating and cooling in your garage design. In addition, adequate ventilation is important for safety and a pleasant work environment.

Let's get one heating and cooling solution out of the way immediately—do NOT tie your garage into the home climate control system. In many places, this is against the law, and for very good reasons. Think about all of the toxic materials you generally keep in the garage. Then think about what your garage smells like after you use things like paint remover and gear oil. How would you and your family feel about the house smelling like your garage?

Whatever solution you use in your garage, the climate control system must be self-contained. This is not only a safe solution, but it's also more cost efficient. No matter how much time you spend in your garage, it's probably less time than you spend in the rest of the home. If you only use the heating and air conditioning system when you're working in the garage, the total bill will be much lower than if it is tied into your home system.

INSULATION

The climate control system in your garage won't do much good unless you prepare the entire garage for heating and cooling. When your home was built, the contractor made sure the doors and windows all sealed properly and the home was adequately insulated. Now you need to make sure that your garage is just as nice as your home—okay, maybe better.

To help maintain a comfortable environment and save money, properly insulate the ceilings and walls in your workshop. It's helpful to install weather stripping around doors and windows. The chapter on walls deals with the topic of insulation a little more in depth since most insulation needs to be installed before the walls are closed in.

Insulation stripping made of foam is easy to install around your windows. Feel around the edges of your windows to determine whether there are drafty spots. If you find a draft, block it off with weather stripping. Simply clean the surface where you'll install the stripping, peel the paper backing, and stick the stripping along the edge of the window.

HEATING SOLUTIONS
Portable Heaters

The most common way to heat a shop is with a portable heater. These include radiant heat, electric, propane, and kerosene heaters. I've used most of these systems and consider all of them temporary solutions. Most of these will keep you sort of warm during December and January.

The biggest problem with the portable units is that they are single-point heaters. In other words, none of them will

This is the air handler for the heat pump. Garage air is pulled in from the bottom of the unit and exhausted at the top. You'll notice that no duct work was used; duct work would have almost doubled the price. This works well for a three-car garage.

distribute the heat around your garage. You'll have one very warm corner in your garage and the opposite wall will be freezing. No matter how many BTUs these heaters put out, you'll still have a distribution problem.

The best solution is to install a ceiling fan to distribute the heat around the garage. This ceiling fan will also keep the garage temperature reasonable during the fall and spring months when you simply need a little circulation.

- **Kerosene heaters.** Heating with kerosene is inexpensive, but kerosene puts out an odor that some people find unpleasant. In addition, kerosene heaters put out a moist heat, which increases the chances for surface rust on any bare metal you might have in your garage, especially when you're using a kerosene heater during the winter when there's a good chance of high humidity.
- **Propane heaters.** Propane is a lot easier to locate than kerosene. You can find propane bottles almost anywhere, including most service stations and convenience stores. Propane heaters generally come in two types. Some have the heating element separate from the tank but connected with a hose. Others mount the heating element directly on the tank. The heaters that are separate tend to be more stable. If you use a tank-mounted heater, place it in a location where it's not likely to get knocked over, especially as the propane begins to run out and the tank gets light.
- **Electric heaters** come in a number of types and sizes. Quartz-element heaters offer the convenience of a replaceable element. Wire-element heaters are usually equipped with a small blower to circulate the heat, so they heat a bigger space more rapidly than propane or kerosene. Ceramic-element heaters are very popular because they are compact, powerful, and efficient. Whichever type of electric heater you choose, don't use aerosol spray paint near it as you could ignite the vapors from the paint.

A TOTAL CLIMATE CONTROL SYSTEM

The best solution for your garage is to install a total climate control system. Treat the garage totally separate from your house with a dedicated heating and cooling system. One solution is to use a heat pump that's coupled with an air conditioning system. The beauty of this system is that it's not much more expensive than a separate heating system and an air conditioner.

The most common, and best, system is referred to as a split system. This is the same arrangement that's found in homes across the country. It consists of a compressor installed outside the garage and a package called an air handler that fits inside your garage.

The thermostat was placed directly on the air handler to save money. In a small garage, the placement of the thermostat is critical, and you can save money by not having to run wire to a remote thermostat.

HEAT PUMP

The heat pump looks just like a split air conditioning system, but it functions as a heater in the winter and an air conditioner in the summer. A heat pump is really just a central air conditioning system that also has the ability to heat your garage during cold weather months.

Think of a heat pump as an air conditioner with a valve that lets it switch between "air conditioner" and "heater." When the valve is switched one way, the heat pump acts like an air conditioner, and when it is switched the other way, it reverses the flow of refrigerant and acts like a heater.

It's called a heat pump because it pumps heat into your garage in the winter, and pumps heat out of your garage in the summer. This ability to both heat and cool makes it an economical and efficient climate control system for your garage. It's a whole lot better than having a kerosene heater sitting around on your garage floor.

How Does This Work?

During summer, this system functions exactly like a standard central air conditioning system, pulling the heat out of your garage and releasing it outside. In winter, it simply reverses the process, extracting the heat that's present in outdoor air and pumping it into your garage.

This is the compressor unit, which lives outdoors. This is also the part of the heat pump that makes noise. Use caution with the placement of this compressor—you don't want it under your bedroom window.

As strange as it may seem, heat is present in all air, even air that's well below freezing. Think of the way your refrigerator removes unwanted heat that accumulates when you open the door and place warm food inside. You can feel that heat coming back into your kitchen from the refrigerator's exhaust fan.

In a similar way, heat pumps remove heat from cold outdoor air and deliver it to your garage to keep you warm and comfortable.

A Supplemental Heater
Heat naturally migrates from warmer to colder areas through windows, doors, ceilings, and walls. Insulation, weather stripping, and caulk slow down this heat loss, but cannot eliminate it. The colder it becomes, the faster your garage loses heat.

The supplemental heater helps the heat pump during weather extremes when a garage may lose heat faster than the heat pump can replace it. Electric heating elements in the unit automatically turn on to make up the difference. Thus, no matter where you live, a heat pump will work.

The downside is that when these supplemental heaters, or electrical grids, are turned on, your electric meter will begin to spin out of control. Heat pumps are really wonderful in North Carolina, but if you live in Minnesota they can force the family budget into Chapter 11 proceedings.

The only salvation is that you don't spend all day and all night in your garage. With a dedicated system, you only need to turn the heat on during the few hours you're playing with your cars. Your local heating/ventilation/air-conditioning (HVAC) contractor can give you a pretty good idea about how this is going to affect the family food budget.

Just Set the Thermostat

Fortunately, heat pumps operate off of thermostats just like your home. This means you can go out to the garage and just turn the heat pump on. Once the temperature reaches the designated level, everything will operate the same way it does for the rest of your house.

Having dealt with far too many kerosene heaters and electric ceramic heaters over the years, I truly appreciate this convenience. I'm sure that the additional money I spent installing a heat pump has been recovered by not going to the local service station weekly to purchase another 5 gallons of kerosene, and the air conditioning is a real plus every August.

SPLIT PORTABLE UNITS

Portable air conditioning units are great for the basic two-car garage. A portable system consists of two components: the cooling unit (placed indoors) and the low-noise, no-drip condenser (placed outdoors), connected by an 11-foot flexible hose with a 3 1/2-inch diameter. This hose fits easily through a small crack in any door or window.

Climate control technology is changing rapidly. Take some time to look at the variety of choices available for your garage.

With the average two-car garage, you're going to need around 13,000 BTUs. You'll spend roughly $2,000 on a split portable unit, but the operating cost will be minimal since you'll at best be operating the system only a few hours a day.

WALL-MOUNTED AND CEILING-SUSPENDED AIR CONDITIONERS

There are several new ways to cool your garage during July and August, including a slim-line universal system that suspends from the ceiling and wall-mounted or floor units. These units are fairly attractive, quiet, efficient, and can be installed by HVAC contractors without the need for air conditioning ducts. A digital wireless LCD remote allows you to display and confirm all controller features and functions from nearly anywhere within a given zone.

The system is comprised of two units: an outdoor condenser and an indoor air handler. The condenser supplies coolant to the air handler through refrigerant lines that run through a small opening in the wall or ceiling and into the back of the unit. The air handler takes in supply air from the room through the front grill and dispenses the newly cooled air back into the room. Special filters are available that promote added humidity control and filtration for certain models.

TO DUCT OR NOT TO DUCT?

If you decide to go with a total climate control system, you'll face the inevitable question concerning ducting the system. In a two- or three-car garage, you really don't need any ducting. Ducting really only serves an aesthetic purpose and will actually detract from your climate control system. You can lose up to 20 percent of your heating or cooling through the ducts. This means you have to insulate your ducts—which translates to more work.

You could treat your garage like an industrial plant and make your duct in 18-inch diameter out of sheet steel and run it directly through the garage. This way any heat, or cool air, will simply go into the garage, and not into the attic. These large circular ducts will also be easy to wipe clean.

AIR FILTRATION

This is the part that made my wife think I had lost total control. I wanted to install an air filtration system in my garage because I hate dirt and I hate the way the garage smells at times. Keep in mind that I already have a total climate control system in my two-car garage. Some of you spend more on wax in a year than I paid for the air filtration system, though, but my wife still doesn't understand that.

Continued on page 90...

This is a room filtration unit for my garage. It can be mounted on a table or hung on the wall. Either way, it takes up very little space.

PROJECT 11 ★

Time: Two to three hours

Tools: Drill, screwdrivers, and standard wiring tools

Talent: ★★   **Tab:** The cost will depend on the size and complexity of the fan you select. They begin at $35 and go into the hundreds.

Tip: Fans that do not include a light will allow for more floor-to-ceiling clearance. That's more important than having additional lights in your garage.

A ceiling fan makes a huge improvement in your garage. In the winter, it helps distribute the heat and in the summer it keeps the cool air flowing. The big problem is finding a place to locate a fan.

Avoiding things like the garage doors will actually be more of a location factor than finding a central location for air circulation. Ideally, the fan should be installed in the center of the garage. You may want several fans if you have a three- or four-car garage.

You don't need a fan with an integral lighting fixture; most are strictly a design feature and not the sort of light we want in our garage. Since a fan draws about the same power as a ceiling light fixture, the electrical circuit shouldn't be overloaded.

Create a new place to hang the ceiling fan rather than replacing an existing light fixture. You'll need to bring electrical power to the fan, but you can tap into an existing circuit to do this. That's no big deal, especially if you have an attic above your garage.

Try to find a location as close to the center of the garage as possible. Next, select a location for the fan in between the ceiling joists to allow for the installation of the electrical junction box. If it's directly next to the joist, drill holes in the side of the electrical junction box and screw it to the joist. (Installation between joists is even better.) Fasten the box to a 2-inch by 4-inch header nailed between the joists. Sometimes you can insert a 2-inch by 4-inch header through the junction box's hole, nailing it to each joist. If that's not possible, you may need to open a larger access hole and patch the hole to close it again.

If you don't mount the fan carefully it could fall on your car. I'm not fond of simply using a junction box to support a ceiling fan. It's far better to use the building structure to support it. Remember, your mounting has to withstand vibration while the fan is running.

The biggest problem with installing a fan in your garage is clearance. Check the floor-to-ceiling height of the fan blades by measuring the floor-to-ceiling distance and subtracting for the part of the fan that will extend below the ceiling down to the lower blade surface. You need an absolute minimum distance of 7 feet between the floor and the fan blade in any garage.

With some models, the fan blade height can be increased with a different mounting arrangement. Remember, though, that you need at least 12 inches between the ceiling and the tops of the fan blades for proper airflow. Having 18 inches is better if the space is available. Take all your measurements before you start the installation process.

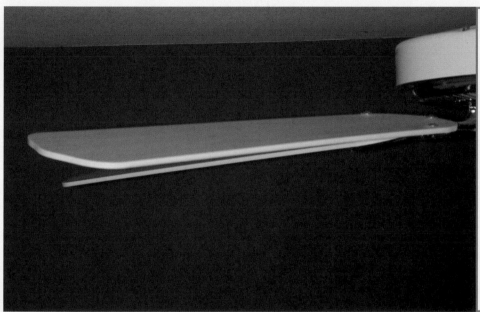

Assemble the fan following the specific instructions that it came with. Regardless of the manufacturer's instructions, if the fan blades are less than a screwdriver's length away from the ceiling, it may be best to install the blades before hanging the fan. It's also best to have 12 to 18 inches between the fan and ceiling for proper circulation. Most fan blades have a two-pronged attachment, using screws that come through holes in the blades and into the flanges. On many fans, you'll find the flanges, or prongs, also need to be mounted to the motor housing. If this is the case, mount them before the flanges are mounted to the blades themselves.

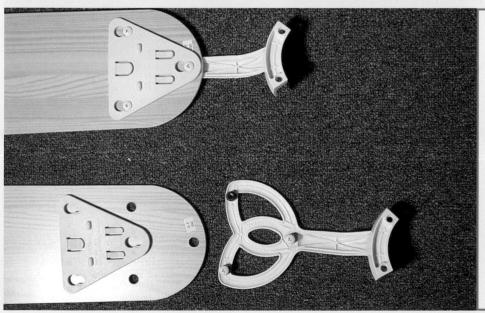

The fan blades are actually mounted in rubber. The fan installation kit includes little rubber mounts and special screws for attaching the blades. Tip: If the fan wobbles when it runs, the blades may be unbalanced. To correct this, try interchanging two adjacent blades. If that doesn't work, take all the blades off and weigh each one on a food or postal scale. If any of the blades is underweight, tape a soft object like detailing clay to the top center of the blade to make its weight the same as the others.

PROJECT 12 ★

Time: Several days

Tools: Sheet metal working tools

Talent: ★★★   **Tab:** $100–500

Tip: Make sure all the ducts are in place before you enclose the ceiling.

Once you've installed a climate control system in your garage you have to get the air distributed around the garage. Ductwork distributes the heat or air conditioned air evenly around your garage. However, not all garages will need duct work. If you have a basic two-car garage, you can probably skip this project. If you have a three- or four-car garage, ductwork will help control the temperature and humidity in your garage.

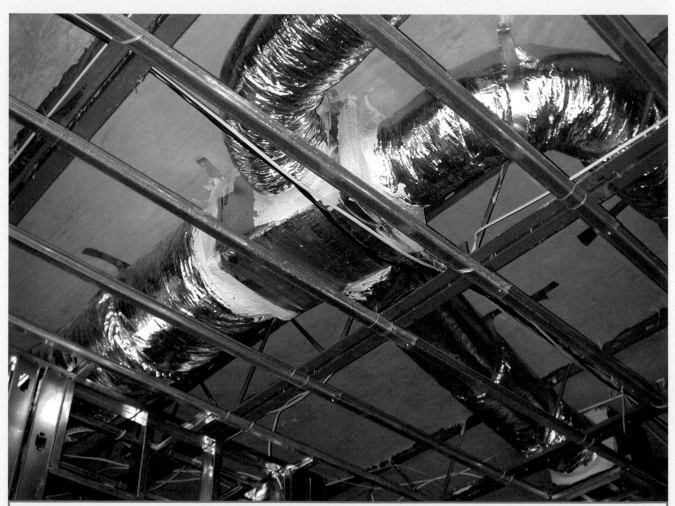

Flexible round ductwork is wonderful. Here's a central junction box for the ducts. Everything is routed into one box and the ducts head off to the corners of your garage. It's as easy to run six vents into your ceiling as it is to run four.

The ducts are suspended from the rafters with large steel straps, making installation easy.

Dismiss any thought about extending the ducts from the home out to the garage. It's probably illegal in your community and is simply not a good idea—the last thing you need is to send car fumes into your living area.

The location of the heating/cooling system plays a critical role in whether or not you need duct work. If you can put the system in a central location there's really no need for ducting your garage.

Another consideration is whether or not your garage has an attic. If you use a system of ducts it's best to install the unit in the actual garage space, not up in the attic. But if it's easy to access the attic, you can put the air handler in the attic to save floor space. Then you simply run a few ducts to outlets in the garage ceiling.

Each of the ducts mounts to a ceiling fixture for a great climate control system in your garage. This flexible round ducting is almost painless to install.

HOW MANY BTUs DO I NEED?

BTU stands for British thermal units. More importantly, it also means how much money you're going to spend heating and cooling your garage.

	Vermont	Virginia
Two-car garage	10,000 BTUs	7,500 BTUs
Three-car garage	15,000 BTUs	12,000 BTUs

Let's take a minute and see what the difference between insulated and non-insulated means for you.

	Vermont (no insulation)	Virginia (no insulation)
Two-car garage	16,000 BTUs	13,000 BTUs
Three-car garage	24,000 BTUs	19,000 BTUs

Continued from page 85...

With an air filtration system, the air in your garage is constantly circulated. The dirty air passes through a pre-filter that grabs all the big chunks of dirt flying around your garage, including lint, dust, and pollen.

Next, the air passes through a HEPA (High Energy Particulate Air) filter that removes particles as small as 0.3 microns (particles 300 times smaller than a human hair). This filter can even grab bacteria from the air.

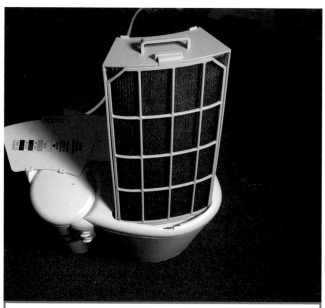

The filter is easy to remove from the unit. They even give you a color-coded picture that explains when you should replace the filter. The dark filter you see in this picture is black foam that can be removed and cleaned in the sink on a weekly basis.

Finally, the air passes through an activated carbon filter to remove any odors in your garage. Activated carbon air filters are really a vast system of pores of molecular size. These pores are highly absorbent with a strong chemical attraction to odorous, gaseous, and liquid contaminants. The filters are usually dark gray and highly porous. They last about a year and cost from $10 to $40 to replace. Most units now have an indicator light that lets you know when it's time to replace the filter.

It may be cheaper to simply buy a new air purifier unit every year. The companies that produce these units have discovered the same thing that Hewlett Packard and Epson discovered about the ink in your ink-jet printer. If they sell these filtration units cheaply enough more people will buy them and they can sell more filters. The profit is in the filter replacement market.

CARBON MONOXIDE DETECTOR

Carbon monoxide detectors may seem a little silly, but they're so cheap, there's no reason you shouldn't have one. If your family hasn't complained about the smell of car exhaust in the house then you don't own any old cars. Unlike a smoke alarm, you don't need a carbon monoxide alarm at several places around the house. Buy one and place it in your garage, but keep in mind that the alarm could be triggered by starting your car.

You can mount the detectors anywhere on a wall, and most plug right into an electrical outlet; just make sure you can hear the alarm. A low level of carbon monoxide is about 40 parts per million. You probably wouldn't feel any effect from that. A high level is about 400 parts per million, and it's potentially life-threatening.

If you're heating your garage with either a kerosene heater or a propane heater, these detection units are really

CLIMATE CONTROL

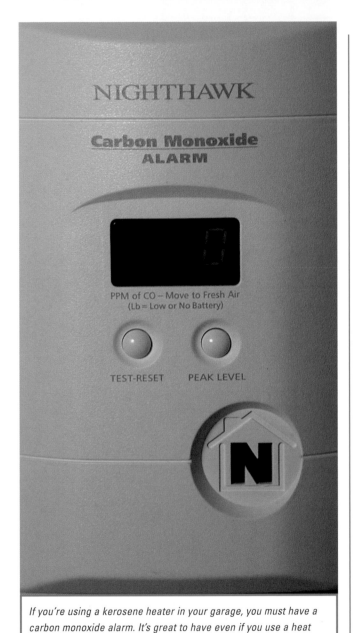

If you're using a kerosene heater in your garage, you must have a carbon monoxide alarm. It's great to have even if you use a heat pump. At the very least, it lets the family know that if you're doing something very stupid in the garage they should open the garage doors before you expire.

RESOURCES

Heat Pump Centre
www.heatpumpcentre.org
This is a good introduction to heat pump technology that doesn't push a specific product, but instead explains how heat pumps work.

How Stuff Works
www.howstuffworks.com
This is a great site for understanding air conditioning and heating systems. Once you get a basic understanding of the basics, you can make some informed choices. They have tutorials on both heat pumps and air conditioning.

a necessity. If there's a high level of carbon monoxide in your garage, open the garage doors and leave them open until the carbon monoxide level returns to normal. Two carbon monoxide alarms that did well in *Consumer Reports* tests are the $50 Senco Model One and the $45 Kiddie Nighthawk Premium Plus. Carbon monoxide alarms should be replaced every five years, so you'll spend about $10 a year to know the level of carbon monoxide in your garage.

CHAPTER 9
WALL AND CEILING TREATMENTS

Every garage has at least three walls and a ceiling. The fourth wall usually consists of large doors so we won't worry about that one right now. Because most people don't really get into their garages, the builder can cut costs and focus on the exterior side of the garage wall rather than the interior.

Garage walls are actually quite important since they're a major area for storage. If you look around your current garage, you'll notice how much stuff you already have stored on the walls. The only thing left to do is make the walls look nice and devise an appropriate storage system that makes maximum use of the space.

Garage walls come in two flavors. There's the garage that is built out of sticks (2x4 framing lumber), and there's the garage that's constructed from concrete blocks. Each one has its own advantages and disadvantages, none of which really matter to you since you already have your garage. You have what you have so let's make the most of it.

If you have a wooden garage, you'll first concentrate on covering the framing. You want to create a wall that will reflect a lot of light and allow for storage. In the first chapter, we talked about thinking of your garage in three dimensions. Now you need to think of your walls as vertical storage space.

INSULATE THE WALLS

Insulation is important regardless of where you live. If you're in Texas, you'll want to keep the cool air in and the hot air out. If you live in Montana, the main concern is how to keep the heat inside the building and the arctic wind out.

Vinyl spackling has a drying time of one hour or more depending on the thickness of the application. You'll need to allow longer for deeper cracks and crevices. Conventional joint compound has a drying time of 8 to 24 hours depending on the thickness of application.

PAPER TAPE

The obvious solution is to use the large rolls of insulation available from your local home center. The rolls are designed to fit in between the studs of your garage walls and can be purchased complete in various thicknesses (for various levels of insulation) with a vapor barrier.

As with most other things in my life, I have a tendency to get carried away with insulation. The price difference between an R18 roll of insulation and a roll rated at R28 is not very significant. Remember, the higher the R number the greater the insulating quality. An R28, while slightly more expensive, will provide more insulation against heat and cold than an R18. You'll only do this job once, and you won't need to purchase a lot of insulation. Why not get carried away and install R28 in all the walls?

Also keep in mind that you'll most likely install a complete climate control system in your garage. Even if it doesn't get all that cold in your area, it probably gets a little warm in the summer and insulation will keep your garage cool in July and August. During part of the year, we want to keep the heat out of our garages, while during other parts of the year, we want to keep the heat in our garages. Insulation does both.

WALL COVERING OPTIONS

Wall covering options, while limited, are far greater than they first appear. Keep in mind that in the average garage, most of your storage will be on the walls so you won't actually see the walls, but rather your storage system.

If your garage is wood framed you'll most likely use drywall over the framing since it's the easiest way to cover the framing. Drywall can also be painted a bright white to reflect the light. The most difficult part of covering the walls is that the ceiling will also need to be covered. Installing drywall on the ceiling isn't that difficult, but you'll need help because the sheets are large.

Remember that if you install drywall on your walls and ceiling, you're never getting back into those areas again, at least not without a lot of trouble. Make sure that you have everything in place before you start enclosing your walls.

Continued on page 97…

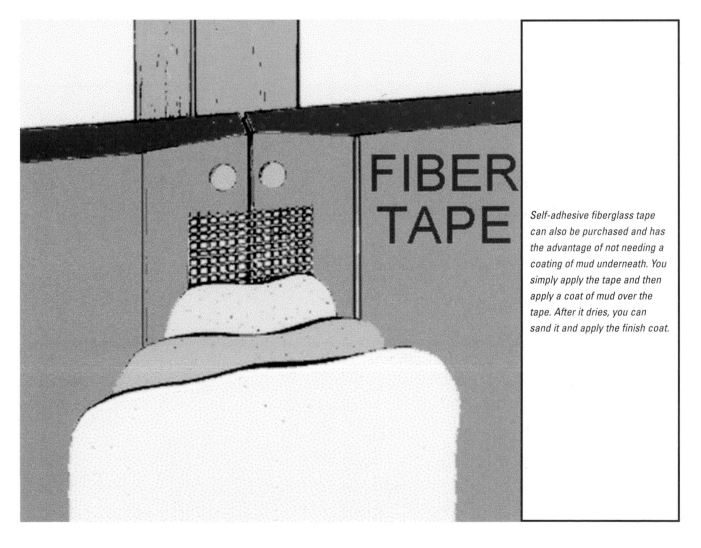

Self-adhesive fiberglass tape can also be purchased and has the advantage of not needing a coating of mud underneath. You simply apply the tape and then apply a coat of mud over the tape. After it dries, you can sand it and apply the finish coat.

PROJECT 13 ★

Time: Several days

Tools: Trowels, buckets, screw guns

Talent: ★★ **Tab:** $100–800

Tip: Installing drywall is a big job. It's not complicated, just tremendously time-consuming and messy. A lot of planning and thought has to go into this project. It's best to work with a friend who's done all of it before.

I'm going to use the generic term "drywall" when referring to gypsum board. You'll also hear called it "wallboard" or by the brand name "sheetrock." They are all made of a gypsum core with a coarse paper on the back and a smooth paper on the finish side.

Drywall sheets come in 4x8 feet, 4x10 feet, 4x12 feet, and even larger. I recommend that you stick to 4x8 sheets; they're easier to work with. Use 1/2-inch drywall for ceilings and walls with 16-inch on-center framing. Use 5/8-inch drywall if your garage has 24-inch on-center framing.

The most important part of the job isn't the drywall itself but rather that you're sure all your work inside the walls is complete. All of the electrical work, duct installation, and insulation have to be finished before you seal the walls up. Think of it like the Egyptians sealing a tomb—once you seal the wall you're not going back in for minor adjustments.

If you had to acquire a building permit, have an inspection done on your mechanical work before you install the drywall. You must make sure your work complies with all

If your garage is constructed of concrete blocks you'll need to install small furring strips for the drywall. This is also a good time to see if your garage walls are truly at a right angle to the floor. Take a little extra time to shim the furring strips so that your new walls will be perfectly flat and smooth.

With drywall you can simply run electrical lines down the wall without having to use conduit. However, if you do that make sure you install nail blockers. The metal plates will keep you from running a drywall screw right into your nice new wires, and in many cases they may be part of your community's electrical codes.

Trim molding is a wonderful thing. The openings around your doors only need to be approximate. When everything is done this huge gap will be covered with molding strips. The same thing applies to electrical boxes and ceiling lights. Get everything as close as you can but don't be obsessed with the fit.

building codes. Inspectors have very little mercy if they show up to inspect your electrical work and find it all sealed behind the drywall.

If you have unfaced insulation batts in your exterior walls, put up a vapor barrier to prevent moisture from condensing inside your walls. In colder climates, the vapor barrier goes between the insulation and the drywall; in warm climates, it goes between the sheathing and the insulation to keep it dry during warm weather.

The final step is to make sure that all the studs and joists are straight, secure, and spaced properly. The nailing faces should be flush and aligned in a level plane. If some of the studs are bowed or crooked you may have to replace them.

Cross furring strips can correct some uneven surfaces in the existing framing. There should be nailing strips at every corner, on both sides of vertical corners and headers. No edge of drywall should go unsupported for more than 2 feet.

If a pipe or wire runs through a hole in a framing member and the hole is within 1 1/4 inches of the edge of the wood, place a metal protective plate along the edge of the wood. This keeps drywall screws and nails from puncturing the pipe or cable and is a code requirement in most areas.

How Much Stuff Do I Need?
I try to keep my trips to the store to a minimum, although for me "a minimum" is a couple times a day if I'm in the middle of a big project. You can minimize these trips by making careful estimates.

You can install electrical junction boxes directly into the concrete blocks prior to installing the drywall. Chisel out a slot in the block and insert the box into the wall. Make sure that the edge of the box will meet the surface of the finished drywall.

Things to Learn Before You Go Shopping

Taping compound is used for the tape coat. It's stronger and coarser than the compounds used for the finishing process.

Topping compound is thinner and finer. It's used for the fill and finish coats and for texturing.

All-purpose compound is halfway between a taping and a topping compound. It comes pre-mixed and is a good choice for do-it-yourselfers.

Chemical compounds come in powdered form only. They are generally very strong and difficult to sand. Most do-it-yourselfers won't want to use chemical compounds.

Ring shank nails hold into wood and prevent "popping" later on. Standard length is 1 1/4 inches for 1/2-inch drywall, and 1 3/8 inches for 5/8-inch drywall.

Drywall screws require the use of a screw gun. Use 1 1/4-inch screws with 1/2-inch drywall and 1 5/8-inch screws with 5/8-inch drywall.

Taping knives are used to get a smooth, tapered joint. For the first "tape coat" you'll need a taping knife that's 5 or 6 inches wide. With each of the next two coats you'll want the knife to cover 1 or 2 inches further in each direction. This means you'll need both an 8- to 10-inch knife and a 12- to 14-inch knife.

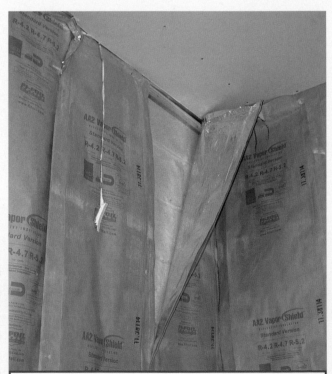

Once you have the furring strips in place, you can install insulation. We've installed a minimal amount of insulation since this garage is in the South. If you're in a colder climate, you may want to use 2x4 studs for furring and double the amount of insulation.

To estimate the number of sheets of drywall you'll need, first determine the total square footage of walls and ceilings. Don't subtract anything for doors and windows, and add 10 percent for a waste allowance.

Now divide the total square footage by 32 if you're using 4x8-foot sheets (40 for 4x10-foot sheets, 48 for 4x12-foot sheets). Round up for any remainders.

Let's consider the average garage to be 20x20 with a 10-foot ceiling. You'll only cover three walls since the garage door is at one end of the box.
• Ceiling: 400 square feet
• Walls: 600 square feet

You'll need at least 1,000 square feet of drywall for a standard 20x20 garage, which works out to roughly 32 sheets of drywall. For every 1,000 square feet of drywall, buy:
• 370 feet of joint tape
• 140 pounds of ready-mixed joint compound
• 700 screws
• 700 nails

Continued from page 93...

DRYWALL

Drywall is a great way to cover all the framing studs, electrical connections, and piping that hide inside your garage wall. You can even use drywall to replace cracked plastered ceilings without the challenge of smoothly covering a ceiling with plaster.

Drywall is commonly available in 4x8 and 4x12 sheets in thicknesses of 3/8 inch, 1/2 inch, and 5/8 inch. A 5/8-inch thickness is recommended for the ceiling. You should check the local building codes for the right materials.

Hanging drywall doesn't require a lot of technical skill. In fact, a good tape job can hide a lot of mistakes. After installing a couple of boards, you'll be able to move right through this project. When you install drywall on the ceiling, a second person will be essential. Also, before you begin hanging drywall you must first check for obstructions.

Drywall Basics

- Don't force drywall into a tight area. You will crush the drywall and create taping problems.
- Always install the ceiling drywall before installing the walls.
- Lay the panels flat on the floor until you're ready to use them, to avoid bending and breaking them. Do not lean them against the wall.
- Make sure the blade on your utility knife is sharp to avoid tearing.
- Hang drywall with a minimal number of seams. The taping will go faster and the result will look a lot better.
- Recruit the help of a friend. This job will take at least two people.

Drywall Mistakes

- Neglecting to make provisions for insulation, ventilation, moisture control, and wiring prior to the installation of drywall.
- Neglecting to install nail guards where wires or pipes run within the studs so that nails or screws will not penetrate.
- Contaminating the compound with debris or dried chips of compound.
- Not having insulation and utilities inspected (check local code) before covering with drywall.
- Not sanding between layers of drywall compound.
- Driving nails so deep that they break the paper on the panels.
- Not using drywall nails.
- Not sanding the final coat of compound to a smooth finish.
- Not butting two panels of drywall at the beveled edge.
- Damaging the edges of the panels during installation.
- Not completely covering the tape with compound.
- Not applying the ceiling drywall before applying the drywall on the walls.
- Not butting sheets at a stud or rafter.

- Applying the drywall sheets with the wrong side exposed.
- Creating more seams than are absolutely necessary by using small scraps.

THE CEILING

You have two choices for a ceiling. The first is to install drywall and finish the ceiling to match the walls. The second option is to use a drop ceiling with panels. Each has its advantages, but a drywall ceiling has a higher-quality, finished look.

Begin with determining the placement of the lights. Everything you do will be a lot easier if you decide on the type and placement of your lights before selecting the type of ceiling you want. If you choose to drywall your garage, remember that the ceiling is the starting point.

Once it's installed, the suspended ceiling offers a lot more flexibility than drywall. You'll be able to change your lighting placement around a few years from now if your needs change. A suspended ceiling conceals obstructions attached to the underside of the joists, yet allows easy access for fixing pipes or adding wiring later on. Suspended ceilings are also better sound barriers than drywall ceilings. And since you level the ceiling as you install it, the existing ceiling joists need not be level or even straight.

With a suspended system, you can add insulation and install ceiling lights by simply removing an acoustical panel and replacing it with a special drop-in fluorescent fixture. You can even add a drop-in with a built-in heating element. Moving panels within the grid is a lot easier than cutting and patching a drywall ceiling.

The biggest part of the job is installing the metal framework for the ceiling tiles. Installing either a tile or suspended ceiling in a 9- by 12-foot room will require 14 to 20 work hours, longer if unusual situations arise. The actual tile installation will take just over an hour. This job is best done by two people since the framework flexes and bends as you install it. Ceilings aren't just for looks; they can also muffle noise and support lights.

Suspended ceiling problems are often caused by:

- Not planning the ceiling layout on paper first.
- Failing to plan grids so they don't run into posts or columns.
- Measuring the ceiling height from a sloping floor, thus creating a sloping ceiling.
- Not laying out runners so that border tiles will be greater than half a tile.
- Not making absolutely certain that the runners are level.
- Allowing the tiles to get dirty during installation.
- Not doing all the rough electrical work for the ceiling light fixtures before installing the ceiling.

- Failing to check that you have space between your ceiling joists and the ceiling light fixtures.
- Failing to correct any ceiling leaks prior to installing the new ceiling.
- Applying loose-filled or rolls of insulation directly on top of the ceiling panels rather than in ceiling joist cavities.
- Having the border tiles on opposing sides of the room unequal.

SIZING JUNCTION BOXES IN YOUR WALL

Once you have the drywall on the studs, it's too late to make changes. An undersized junction box can be an absolute nightmare. Make some basic drawings and select the appropriate size wire (see Chapter 6). All switches and outlets (receptacles) need a properly sized junction (electrical) box. For example, a 2-inch by 3-inch box with three wires (14-gauge) should be 2 1/2 inches deep. The same box with five wires must be 3 1/2 inches deep.

Installing an undersized box is probably the most common wiring mistake for do-it-yourselfers. When in doubt, it's usually best to use a larger box. If you're not sure about box size requirements, remember to ask your electrical inspector when submitting diagrams. Remember, it's important to follow the local electrical code.

Here's one way to calculate minimum box size:

- Count the number of wires for the box. Don't count outlet/switch pigtails, and count all ground wires as one.
- Take that number and add one for each cable clamp and two for each device (like a switch or outlet).
- If the box contains only 14-gauge wires, multiply the total by 2 cubic inches. Or, for 12-gauge wires, multiply the total by 2.25 cubic inches.
- The result is the minimum allowable volume the box should be. Volumes are usually stamped into the back of the box on the inside.

That said, there is an easier way—just put the deep junction boxes in every location. The total increase in cost will be less than $10 for the whole garage.

SLOTTED WALL PANELING

You see slotted wall paneling in every shopping center you visit. Retail stores love the flexibility this type of wall provides for displays. Think of slotted wall paneling as an alternative to ordinary pegboard rather than an alternative to shelving. Like pegboard, the panels can't hold a lot of weight and are better for organization than storage.

Slotted wall paneling comes in a variety of colors that can add a dash of brightness to an otherwise drab garage wall. The panels come in easy-to-use sheets that measure 48 inches wide by 15 inches high by 1 1/16-inch thick.

These panels can run up a sizable bill very quickly. If you want to do the side wall in your garage, you'll spend around $1,000. That means you have a thousand-dollar wall that can't really be used for anything but light storage.

There are three ways to attach these panels to your garage wall. You can screw right through the slot provided in the panel. Locate the position of the bottom panel and fasten it to the wall by drilling through the slots in the panel into wall studs or blocking. Add the next panel and repeat the procedure on up the wall.

Slotted wall paneling is becoming so popular that the Whirlpool Corporation has introduced the Gear Wall. This was designed as a total garage system so you can hang everything possible on these walls, including cabinets.

Gear Wall panels are constructed from a composite material and are designed to endure the heat, cold, and humidity of the garage. The 1-foot-high by 8-foot-long tongue-and-groove panels attach over drywall or directly on wall studs with screws. The Whirlpool wall paneling system runs $8.75 per square foot. That means to cover the rear wall of your two-car garage you will spend approximately $1,500. All of a sudden drywall looks cheap.

Also remember that basic hooks for the wall panel system can cost from $10 to $15 per hook. This system can get really expensive really fast. A 48-inch shelf is $50. Estimate how many feet of shelving you have in your garage and you'll hit a substantial number very quickly.

The advantage of this system is the total flexibility. If you cover your wall with the Gear Wall, you can reorganize your whole garage in a matter of hours. When you combine the wall sections with the associated items, there's nothing on the market that gives you such flexibility.

Visit the Whirlpool website (www.whirlpool.com) and play with the Whirlpool planner. You should even be able to do some cost calculation on the planner.

The baked-on finish of these wall panels makes cleaning simple with paper towels and a bottle of Windex. Of all the wall options, slotted paneling is without a doubt the easiest to keep clean.

THE FOURTH WALL—THE GARAGE DOOR

Garage doors are really in their third generation of existence. Wood was the material of choice in the first generation of doors. About 20 years ago, insulated, steel garage doors appeared. Nowadays, fiberglass and other composites are bringing about further change and advancements. A fiberglass outer skin in garage doors allows you to duplicate the look of natural wood on a surface that otherwise would appear very plain. If your door faces the street, a stainable, fiberglass door may be ideal for you.

Most of the older garage doors allow wind and wind-blown rain to enter the garage. Today, a tongue-and-groove feature is used on the edge of most doors. Some doors

Continued on page 102…

PROJECT 14 ★

Time: Up to one day

Tools: Electric screwdriver and drill

Talent: ★★★   **Tab:** $200–1000

Tip: Think carefully about how much wall paneling you need. This paneling can't hold a great deal of weight. It would be a shame to cover all this expensive paneling with huge shelving units.

Slotted wall paneling is one of those great little ideas borrowed from retail store displays. It's an alternative to traditional pegboard, and it allows you to hang more stuff on your wall.

Whirlpool (the washing machine people) has ventured into garage systems big-time. Their whole product line is based on the slotted wall panel system. The beauty of the system is that it can be installed right over existing walls.

Appearance is the biggest asset of wall paneling. It's easy to keep clean because of the smooth surface. Cleaning your garage wall consists of simply removing everything from the wall and wiping it down with an all-purpose cleanser. You'll need to do this every few months since the slots hold a lot of dirt and dust.

There are some significant disadvantages to wall paneling that need be considered. The first one is the price—to cover the rear wall in a two-car garage may cost hundreds of dollars. The walls in your garage could easily end up costing more than the flooring.

The most serious consideration, though, is the amount of weight that these walls can hold. While it may look pretty, wall paneling may not hold up under the sort of weight we like to put on our shelves. Add framing strips if you have

a concrete block wall. This would also be a good time to add insulation between the paneling and block wall if you live in the North.

All sorts of hooks and brackets are available for slotted wall panels, but they won't hold the kind of weight that some of us put on our garage shelves. Be cautious when putting any substantial weight on these walls. Garage Tek uses a locking system for the shelving.

Check the available credit on your Visa card before you create this sort of garage. Notice how the white panels reflect light around the garage. Also notice that the slotted wall paneling allows everything thing to be off the floor. Cleaning this garage floor just became very easy. Garage Tek

WALL AND CEILING TREATMENTS

99

PROJECT 15 ★

Time: Less than one day

Tools: Saw, drill and screwdriver

Talent: ★★   **Tab:** Under $25

Tip: Consider using several small pegboards rather than a single large one. This give you a lot more flexibility in arranging your garage.

We've all used pegboard before, but very few of us have been happy with this solution. The biggest advantages of pegboard storage are that everything is both visible and easily accessible. The bad part is that the pegboard can become one giant dirt collector. After a few years things get very nasty looking.

This project designs a pegboard unit that will not only allow easy access but be movable. The entire unit can be removed from the wall and moved to another part of the garage.

Since the idea is to make this unit portable you can start with a very basic 2-foot by 4-foot piece of pegboard. A pegboard has very little strength so we've added a frame designed to keep the pegboard from curling. Too often the weight of the items causes the board to warp. Using a series of 2-foot by 4-foot pegboards rather than a larger single unit will help combat warping.

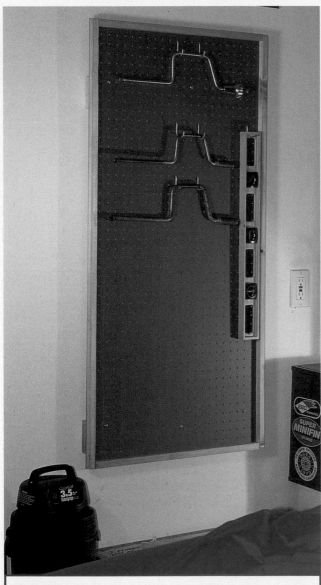

Pegboard is a handy way to store a number of items. In this particular project, the pegboard can be easily removed from the wall for cleaning and painting.

A mounting strip is screwed to the wall to allow us to hang the pegboard on the wall without permanently attaching it.

You'll need a table saw to cut the mounting strip so that it forms an angle. Here you can see how the mounting system works—the weight of the pegboard forces the unit closer to the wall as the weight increases.

There are a lot of new wall anchors on the market. These are designed for use in drywall. They work much better than the old-style plastic anchor.

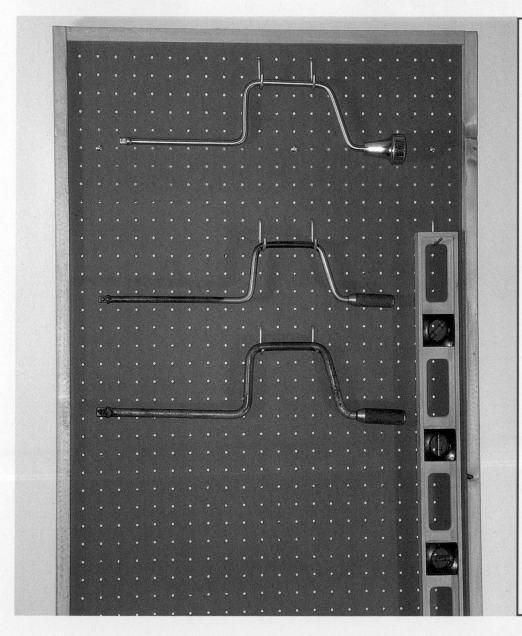

Here is the completed unit. I think you're much better off with a series of small units than one large one. Pegboard has a tendency to collect all the dirt in your garage and is affected by high humidity.

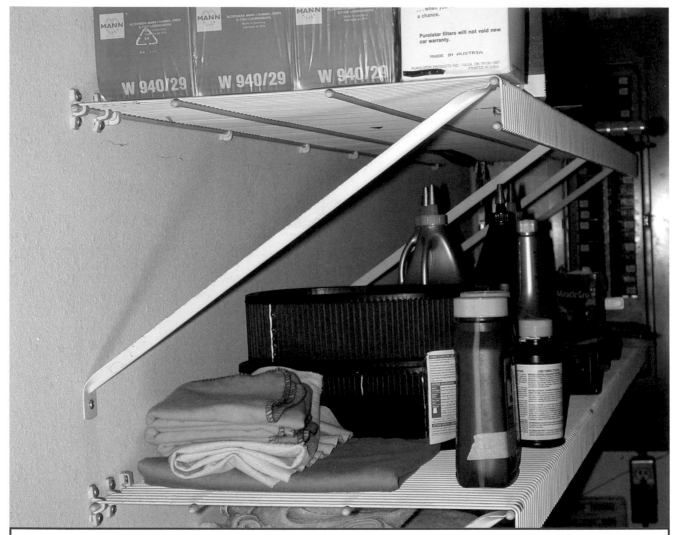

Wire shelves are not only an economical solution, they're also extremely easy to install. Here, the shelves are mounted into a concrete block wall. They come in a variety of widths and can be cut to any length you need. Some home centers now carry shelving with a chrome finish that is easy to wipe clean. If you intend to put heavy items on your shelves, you may want to use more brackets than you see here.

Continued from page 98…

include a weather-strip gasket that seals tightly as the door sections close upon one another.

Security is a big deal for most of us. With standard glass windows, the bad guys can easily see your collection of cars, tools, and motorcycles. New plastic windows are available that act like glass; they allow light to enter but obscure the view into your garage.

You should also worry about radio-controlled garage-door openers. High-tech thieves routinely steal the codes from cellular phones and remote-controlled burglar alarms on cars. This same technology can grab your remote-control garage door code out of thin air. Certain garage-door-opener companies have technology that changes the code every time the door is opened, selecting from billions of code

choices. High-tech thieves will not waste their time at your house if you own such an opener.

When your door is installed, be sure that the company installs a high-quality, bottom-door seal and perimeter weather stripping. Air infiltration is the biggest energy thief in garage doors. Your new, well-insulated door is useless if cold or warm air can easily enter your garage around the edge of the door. Insist on a tight fit.

Your garage door can contribute to high heat loss during the winter. Close the garage door and stand inside the garage on a bright day. If you have light coming in around the garage door, you can be sure you have heat going out.

Garage door installation is not a project you should do yourself. Garage doors are the largest mechanical objects in your house. The springs used to open them can store and

The distance between the shelves can be changed as well.

release deadly force. People are seriously injured and killed each year when they try to install garage doors or perform advanced service on existing doors. The only service you should attempt is the periodic lubrication of the wheels, hinges, and tracks. Use a lightweight oil, not a heavy bearing grease.

RESOURCES

Productive Workspace.com
Scott Machine Tool Company
2780 Bert Adams Rd, Suite 400
Atlanta, Georgia 30339-3926
www.productiveworkspace.com
This is the distributor for GarageWall. The company also carries a complete line of Lista tool cabinets.

Csgnetwork.com
www.csgnetwork.com/dropceilingcalc.html
Here is a wonderful calculator for determining how many pieces you're going to need to create a suspended ceiling. While you're there, look around. They have calculators for just about everything you might imagine. You may want to look at the calculator for how much drywall you'll need and the cost of the entire project.

Professional race shops have the same basic issues that you have in your home garage. Why did they solve the problem that particular way, and how much did it cost? How do these race shops deal with the same issues that you confront? Read on and find out.

ALEX JOB RACING

You could say this is just a two-car garage. But it's really a huge shop that houses two cars in an area larger than most homes. You'll need very specific directions to find this shop. After turning down a country road, you'll find yourself looking at a typical industrial park with a monotonous array of prefabricated buildings. If you blink, you'll miss the big tractor trailer parked along the side of one of the buildings—the only indication you've just arrived at one of the premier Porsche race shops in the world.

Alex Job Racing
551 Southridge Industrial Dr.
Tavares, Florida 32778
www.alexjobracing.com

This wonderful floor—gray enamel floor paint —was cheap and easy to put down. Alex Job moved into the building three years ago and needed flooring that was not only easy to install, but would also allow them to get the shop up and running as quickly as possible. They had a tremendous advantage in that the floor was brand-new concrete.

FLIS MOTOSPORTS

The Flis family grew up in Daytona, so racing was a natural activity. They've been running sports cars at the Rolex 24-Hour race for well over 15 years. During that time, they've built cars for Robby Gordon and Kevin Harvick and they've won the 24-hour race and the season championship. Much like the Alex Job shop, the entire operation is housed in a rather nondescript industrial building built from concrete blocks. It seems the best race teams in the country are often in garages not far removed from what is attached to the average suburban house.

Team Flis
Ormond Beach, Florida
386-672-0099
www.teamflis.com

This is a very serious welder. Porsches are very serious race cars. The beauty of this welder is that it's on wheels and can be moved to the job. Remember, it's not always going to be possible to move the job to the welder.

I'm always looking for little things that can help me stay organized. As you look around the Alex Job Porsche shop, you'll find dozens of muffin tins. Muffin tins from your local grocery store are great for keeping little bolts and small things from getting moved all around your workbench.

How many times have you needed a hydraulic press? They take up very little space on your garage floor and can save you a trip to the machine shop. Just make sure that you get a heavy-duty model that's very stable.

All of us try to make do with what we have around our house or shop. In the case of Alex Job Racing, they needed a hose rack and had a few extra BBS wheels around. A Chevelle wheel would work just as well for your garage.

This area is best described as a workstation; the term workbench really doesn't do it justice. Behind each of the three lifts in the shop is an identical work area. The workbench is integrated into the shelving area. Storage areas surround each workbench.

The bead blasting cabinet is located in the center of the shop for easy access. There are two nice features with this standing cabinet. First, you'll notice that the blasting media can be easily removed via the chute in the center of the cabinet. Second, the area surrounding the blasting cabinet can be easily cleaned. Every single time you remove something from the cabinet you'll get sand on your floor or countertop. It's a lot easier to sweep the floor than to get behind a cabinet that you have on a shelf.

Most race car teams really get into fabricating brackets. This hose rack is a good example of what can be done with minimal materials and a little creativity, and it probably only took five minutes to make.

The best part of the shop is that all the stuff that makes noise is put out back. More and more professional shops are using a back area for compressors and hazardous materials. Even if you can't put your compressor outdoors, you can create a small area for hazardous waste.

All of the tops of the workbenches in the Alex Job shop are heavy steel. They're easy to keep clean and always look nice. Every few weeks, you can sand this top down with 600-grit paper and it'll look just like new. Here we see the ubiquitous Alex Job muffin tins in use once again.

This wheel rack was really the inspiration for the one I built in Chapter 3. A rack like this keeps everything off the floor and makes the shop look a lot neater. The Flis shop has three of these around the shop.

This is what happens if you have a lot of aluminum sheets, a welder, and some spare time. I'm sure it would have been more cost effective to get a dustpan from Wal-Mart, but it would never be as cool.

The Flis team uses a lot of plastic bins. You can use shelves right up against the ceiling to store these plastic bins. They're out of the way, but every bin is clearly labeled and you can easily get them down.

SOME IDEAS FROM PROFESSIONAL SHOPS

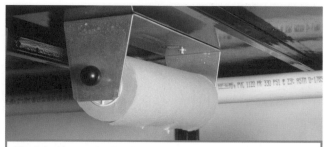

The little things make the difference. If you can fabricate a whole race car how hard can it be to make a paper towel holder? Now, no more rummaging around in the middle of the night; the paper towels are right in front of everyone.

Every single drawer in the pit cart is clearly labeled. The guys on the Flis team use these tools every single day of the week and they still feel the need to label everything. Why shouldn't we do the same thing? We'll spend $50 on a wrench we use once a year, but won't spend $40 on a decent labeling machine. Go figure.

Over the years, I've always installed electrical plugs along the rear of my workbenches. Flis Racing puts the electrical outlets directly on the front of their workbenches. No more reaching over things to get to the plugs. It also keeps you from putting things in front of the outlets all the time, and then having to move them out of the way to reach the outlet.

Here we have the infamous war wagon, or pit cart. This can be hooked up to a golf cart and pulled out to the pits for the next Rolex 24-Hour race, or used in the shop as a toolbox. That means they get double use out of a single item and at 3:00 in the morning at Daytona they know where everything should be.

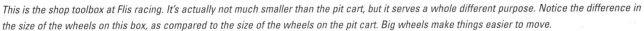

This is the shop toolbox at Flis racing. It's actually not much smaller than the pit cart, but it serves a whole different purpose. Notice the difference in the size of the wheels on this box, as compared to the size of the wheels on the pit cart. Big wheels make things easier to move.

In Chapter 6, I discussed the sort of outlet you need for a serious welder. The last time I counted, Flis Racing had six different welders around the shop. Two giant outlets like this shouldn't be a surprise, then. When you bring this sort of electricity into your home garage you may want to call on a professional electrician.

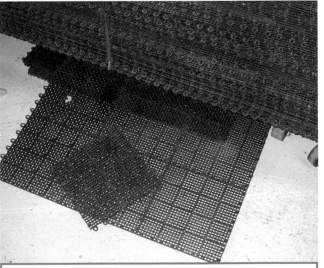

Flis Racing has enough vinyl tile to cover the entire shop, yet they don't use it. The shop floor at Flis is high-quality enamel paint. The vinyl tile is used at the track. Here is over 400 square feet of floor tiling that isn't used in the home shop.

The fit is perfect, although I'm sure the people who made these plastic bins never intended them to be containers for AP brake fluid. I'm equally sure that the AP brake fluid producers didn't size their containers to fit this bin.

Most of us sort out our nuts and bolts by their size. Flis Racing has everything sorted out by its use. It's much easier to locate a bolt for the R. H. Crash Pod than it is to find a $\frac{3}{16}$- by 1-inch bolt in the nut and bolt assortment. Take a compartmentalized tray such as this and divide it into about 20 different sections. Since each section will be very small, you can have a lot of them. This should work as well for the restoration crowd as it does for the racers.

We all have a lot of wire hanging around our garages. Flis Racing has actually organized their wire by size so they can find what they're looking for. You could easily make one of these racks for your home garage. Since most of us purchase wire in 25- or 50-foot rolls, our rack could be a lot smaller. You could also make it out of wood.

Here's the big bolt rack. Again, everything is clearly labeled. While this open arrangement is nice for a professional shop, you should probably consider something enclosed for your home garage. Remember, a professional race team may use more hardware in a week than you'll use in a year. The enclosed arrangement is easier to keep clean.

Acid etching, 28
Additions, 10, 11
Air compressor, 48–50, 67
Air conditioners, 85
Air distribution system, 49
Air filtration, 85, 90
Air handler, 82
Air lines, 33, 50, 51
Air tools, 49
Battery charger, 71
Bead blasting cabinet, 50, 53–55, 67, 106
Bench grinder, 67
Bolt rack, 110
Breaker box, 65
BTU, 90
Cabinets, 36, 37, 43, 47
Car storage, 38
Carbon monoxide detector, 90, 91
Carpet, 20, 21
Ceiling fans, 86, 87
Ceiling, 97
Ceiling, suspended, 97
Circuits, 65, 67
Climate control, 15, 16, 82–91
Color rendering index (CRI), 75, 76
Color temperature, 75
Cooling, 16
Drill press vise, 58
Drill press, 53, 58, 67
Drywall, 93–97
Ducting, 85, 88, 89
Electrical code, 63, 64
Electrical conduit, 70
Electrical grid, 62–72
Epoxy floor, 20, 23, 24, 73
Fire extinguishers, 10
Fire suppression systems, 17
Floor installation, 22, 23
Floor jacks, 29
Floor maintenance, 25–28
Floor plans, 13, 14
Floors, 16
Garage door, 98, 102, 103
Garage pit, 11
Garages, basic large, 14
Garages, monster, 14

Garages, with loft, 14, 15
GFCI, 70, 71, 72
Grinding wheel, workbench, 59
Hammers, 58
Heat pump, 83, 84
Heater, supplemental, 84, 85
Heaters, electric, 83
Heaters, kerosene, 83, 91
Heaters, portable, 82, 83
Heaters, propane, 83
Heating solutions, 82, 83–85
Heating, 16
Hose rack, 105
Hose reel installation, 52, 53
Hydraulic press, 105
Insulation, 82, 92, 93
Interlocking tile, 19, 21
Jack stand, 21, 36
Junction box, 63, 64, 70, 98
Lifts, 13, 48
Light brightness, 74
Light bulb selection, 79, 81
Light color, 75
Light fixtures, 76
Light quality, 74
Lighting, 16, 67, 73–81
Lighting, fluorescent, 75–77
Lighting, general, 74
Lighting, movable, 81
Lighting, natural, 76
Lighting, puck, 77, 80
Lighting, recessed, 76
Lighting, task, 73
Lighting, track, 77, 78, 79, 80
Lighting, workbench, 77, 80
Lights, halogen, 75, 77
Lights, xenon, 80
Moisture, 19–21, 23, 24
New garages, 11, 12
Outlets, 62, 64, 68, 108, 109
Overhead door, 12, 14
Painted floor, 23, 24
Paper towel holder, 108
Parts cleaning tanks, 60, 61
Pegboard, 100, 101

Penske, Roger, 9
Pit cart, 108
Planning, 9–18
Plycerin, 26
Polished floor, 24, 25
Power washing, 26, 27
Restoration parts, 30, 31
Safety, 16
Sheds, 17
Shelves, wire, 102
Shelving, 36, 106
Shelving, adjustable, 37
Shelving, industrial, 31
Shelving, open, 33
Sliding doors, 12, 14
Socket organizer, 32
Sound system, 10
Spackling, vinyl, 92
Spray booth, 56, 57
Spray painting, 53
Stain removal, 25
Storage areas, 16
Storage shed, 12
Storage, 30–39
Storage, attic, 37
Storage, ceiling, 36, 38
Storage, detailer, 33
Storage, racers', 32
Storage, wheel, 34, 35
Surface preparation, 28
Thermostat, 83, 85
Tile, plastic, 20
Tile, removable, 21
Tile, vinyl, 22, 23, 109
Toolboxes, 32, 33, 43, 50, 109
Tools, 48–61
Truss storage system, 39
Vacuum cleaner, 60
Vacuum system, 53, 54, 55, 60
Ventilation, 16
Vise, 61
Wall paneling, slotted, 98, 99
Wall treatments, 92–97
Water supply, 16
Welders, 59, 72, 104
Wheel rack, 107
Wheeled dolly, 21

Wire size, 65, 68
Wiring, 66, 67, 70
Work areas, 16
Workbench construction, 42
Workbenches, 40–47, 107
Workbenches, commercial, 41
Workbenches, home built, 41
Workbenches, metal top, 42
Workbenches, movable, 44, 45
Workbenches, wood top, 41
Workstation, 106
Wrenches, 59

111

**101 Projects for Your Corvette
1984–1996**
ISBN 0-7603-1461-6

**Corvette Restoration Guide
1963–1967**
ISBN 0-7603-0179-4

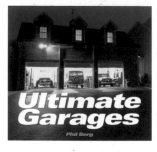

Ultimate Garages
ISBN 0-7603-1471-3

**Monster Garage: How to Customize
Damn Near Anything**
ISBN 0-7603-1748-8

Ultimate Auto Detailing Projects
ISBN 0-7603-1448-9

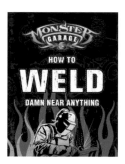

**Monster Garage: How to Weld
Damn Near Anything**
ISBN 0-7603-1808-5

**High-Performance
Handling Handbook**
ISBN 0-7603-0948-5

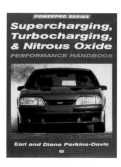

**Supercharging, Turbocharging,
and Nitrous Oxide
Performance Handbook**
ISBN 0-7603-0837-3

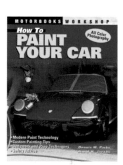

How to Paint Your Car
ISBN 0-7603-1583-3